THE WORLD FOR GOD

Published and Unpublished Writings and Speeches of

EVANGELINE CORY BOOTH

VOLUME II

Compiled by

JOHN D. WALDRON

Published by

THE SALVATION ARMY

LITERARY DEPARTMENT

USA EASTERN TERRITORY

The World for God

Published and Unpublished
Writings and Speeches of

Evangeline Cory Booth

Volume II

by John D. Waldron

© 1992 The Salvation Army, New York

ISBN: 0-89216-096-9

All rights reserved

Published by: The Salvation Army
              Literary Department
              (USA Eastern Territory)
              440 West Nyack Road
              West Nyack, N.Y. 10994-0635

Printed in the United States of America
First Printing--1992

Table of Contents

Chapter Seven: Songs and Poems

Chapter Eight: Personal Glimpses -- Autobiographical

Foreword

Commissioner John D. Waldron (R) has once again bent his indefatigable skills as an anthologist to harvest words from the Army's past. Evangeline Booth, daughter of the Founder and fourth General of The Salvation Army, can still speak direct to the heart. Renowned for her oratory no less than for her dramatic personality and charismatic leadership, Eva Booth in her day swayed the emotions to challenge her hearers and to win the hearts of thousands for the Lord. She was an outstanding woman of God.

To have value for us today, words from the past must do more than inform our minds or even warm our hearts. Therefore any Army anthology should not merely lead us into a nostalgia for the past but spur us forward in the cause of Christ.

Eva Booth herself reminds us: "We Salvationists care little for tradition. The past, good as it may have been in conquest and victory, is incomparable with the mighty present and future. It is not to unlock the doors of the barred and finished past that our hearts pine for, but rather to insert the key of unflagging, tireless zeal in the golden lock of opportunity that the future places before us."

Therefore, in commending to your interest and profit General Eva Booth's words, I pray that your zeal and devotion to Christ may be kindled anew. Jesus, who is the same yesterday and forever, is our Lord; our inspiration, today and into the future.

General Eva Burrows

Introduction

When it was suggested by the USA Eastern Territorial Literary Council that we might compile a volume of selected writings by General Evangeline Cory Booth, the task seemed relatively easy.

Her several published books are on my bookshelves, and choice quotations abound, ripe for the compiler's plucking. My modest library, together with my files, offered scores of pages of the writings of this eloquent and dynamic daughter of The Salvation Army's revered cofounders.

Then I began to explore other sources, and I found myself overwhelmed. In The Salvation Army National Archives, then located in Verona, N.J. I discovered six volumes of *War Cry* articles from her 30 years in the United States, with more than 250 articles covering 1966 pages of typescript. Listings alone for other file holdings ran to many pages. Two boxes containing scores of priceless sermon notes kept me enthralled. Boxes of letters and documents provided intimate insight into her mind and heart over the long years of her life, from early officership until past retirement.

The USA Western Territory shared a handwritten set of Training College lectures from her very early years in England and Canada. The George Scott Railton Center in Toronto provided valuable photos and writings from her years of leadership in that territory, as well as important material on Army international affairs and personal glimpses of her children. The School for Officers' Training in Suffern, N.Y. discovered and provided many volumes of typescript not found elsewhere.

Finally, wallowing in thousands of pages of print and pen, I realized that the project had grown far beyond our initial expectations, and the Literary Council proposed that two volumes would be needed to provide even a sampling of the incredible output of her heart and mind.

Months have been spent in reading and deciding what should be left out to keep the books within manageable proportions. We now offer a rather limited distillation of Evangeline Booth's speeches, articles, lectures, sermons, letters, poems and documents. Through them, the reader will catch something of the vision, dynamism and eloquence of this brilliant leader.

A bibliography has been provided for those who are interested in reading further about her life, and this is encouraged. However, we have also provided two brief biographical sketches to introduce her to a new generation of readers: one written at the time of her appointment to Canada, in her very early officership; the other at the time of her promotion to Glory.

The reader is also encouraged to secure the cassette of her voice, in her great lecture, "The World's Greatest Romance." Although recorded in the days of primitive equipment, the quality of her eloquence comes through, and will add a whole new dimension to your understanding of this remarkable woman. The cassettes may be secured from the Trade Departments of the various United States territories.

The compiler's heartfelt thanks are extended to Lt. Colonel William D. MacLean, Literary Secretary, and the

USA Eastern Territory Literary Council, for their guidance and encouragement; to Connie J. Nelson and Susan Sherlock- Mitchem, archivists at the National Archives and Research Center, now located in Alexandria, Virginia; to Major William L. Brown, Director of the George Scott Railton Center in Toronto, and his staff, for valuable assistance; to Colonel Ronald Irwin, for supplying copies of lecture notes; to Major Lorraine Sacks, Librarian at the School for Officers' Training in Suffern, N.Y. for helpful assistance.

At the National Archives, I came across an obscure reference to Evangeline's name, and the quotation forms an appropriate introduction to these volumes. It is taken from undated sermon notes on "Not Well Pleased," in which she lists the books she had read in her youth, including: "*Uncle Tom's Cabin*--(the Eva I was named after). I read it many times over, and it made a mark upon my whole character, making me more careful to be gentle and kind and considerate, most attractive qualities, to those under me--which principles I have endeavored to put into practice until this present day."

J.D.W.

Chapter One
The Life and Ministry of Jesus Christ

The Christ of the Doorstep

Behold, I stand at the door, and knock: if any man hear my voice, and open the door, I will come in to him, and will sup with him, and he with me Revelation 3:20).

From The War Cry (New York), December 3, 1921.

This text reveals to our minds a vision of Christ which is one of the most beautiful presented in the Bible.

As we read, our eyes rest upon Him as we saw Him in the picture-books of childhood. The tall, slender, delicate form, with a countenance of faultless beauty--the faultless beauty of blameless purity--standing at the door. And it is a closed door!

The picture impresses me first with the universally recognized fact that with all dwellings, no matter how resplendent with architectural achievement, or how lowly in crude and impoverished appearance, it is the door that is the acme of importance.

It is the door that shuts out the enemy, the door that opens to the friend. It is at the door the workman lays down his tools. It is at the door the traveler shakes from his garments the dust of the day's journey. It is the door that stands ajar for the girl or the boy who has wandered.

It is the door of my own home that comes before me as I write, my father and mother upon its threshold, their arms locked like the interlacing branches of a great oak, keeping all the hurt and harm from within. Sometimes father

2

opened it to us, but oftenest mother, when we returned merry from the game, or with bleeding finger or scratched knee. I see her now like an angel awaiting our entrance, her voice, as she called our names, as sweet as the chantings that broke over Bethlehem.

Ah! I have grown up since then. I have passed in and out of some of the world's most magnificent entrances, but no door like that door. Angels encamped about it, and as I write, all the tender memories, lights and shadows, joys and sorrows, losses and affections, with their height and depth and length and breadth and eternity of meaning coming down to me through the years, I find laden with the blessings of that doorstep. Let all the hosts of heaven sing the praises of God forever for the Christ of the Doorstep!

I learn again from the picture that God is near at hand. He is quite close. We have not to travel a long way to find Him. So many of us, if we want to meet or talk with our friends, or even our relations, father or mother or child, have to take a long journey.

A minister's little boy of four years of age, on his way home one Sabbath, after hearing his father preach on the text, "Blessed are the pure in heart," asked the question, "Where is God, father?" "In heaven," the minister replied. "When you took me just over to Uncle Harry's farm you had to carry me most of the way, so it is quite certain I shall never see God." Since then he has learned, and is preaching to the heathen on the missionary fields, that God is quite near--nearer than Uncle Harry. We need not even lift our voices when we speak to Him. He can hear a whisper. He can hear what is lower than a whisper, for He says: "Before they call I will answer."

How, in our ignorance, we blunder, and how we suffer through our blunders! If we could but learn our lessons without making so many mistakes!

Some of us think there must of necessity be a toilsome journey to travel to reach this great, all-saving, all-helping, all-redeeming God. That there must be some great expense of money, of effort or of learning, many years spent in scientific research.

Some of us think we must attack every positive of God with a negative; that we must refute infinite plan and arrangement with finite reasoning and questioning, and see if the great unerring Creator can stand the test of the little, insignificant creature; if the sun can withstand the glimmer of the rush light. So we travel along making these big mistakes.

Some of us think we must travel the long, toilsome journey of good deeds--sewing for the poor, nursing the sick. Some, that we must sacrifice, and even some that we must do penance or submit to physical suffering.

All these things may be good and helpful. A great number of them are very desirable and very blessed. I say to those who have given their mite or their cup of cold water, go on! The only change I would suggest is that you make it more and give it oftener. The service you have rendered others will, of all that has to do with earth, be the thing you will care most to think upon when you are dying. But no service or suffering or sacrifice or knowledge will of itself bring Jesus into your heart with His peace and happiness and salvation.

Christ does not stand at the end of the avenues of service or scientific research or years of sacrificial deeds or

4

a long period in the theological seminary. In fact, we often become so absorbed in our own righteous productions, so concentrated upon the development of our own reputation, so elated over the promulgation of our own ideas as to rights and wrongs, and laws and justice, so fascinated because of the thousand questions we can ask more than the ordinary man as to God's sovereignty, Christ's divinity and the eternal decrees that, like Saul of Tarsus, after sitting at the feet of Gamaliel, the greatest religious teacher of his day, we miss Jesus altogether.

We are running with heated thirst and quickened feet down those mistaken avenues to find Him, when, to the everlasting joy of the hosts of all the redeemed on earth and in heaven, He stands upon our threshold, upon our doorstep, at our door!

So simple! We cannot be saved as philosophers, but as little children. We cannot go to heaven by the way of Athens, but by the way of Bethlehem. Not by the Mars Hill of reason, but by opening the door of the heart.

O sinner! Christ is near you. Throw out your arms in repentance now, and the first thing you will strike will be a beam, and that beam will be the Cross.

Again, I learn from the text that Christ is not only within the most limited reach, but that with humility infinite He stands upon our own level--on our doorstep. Think of it!

He might have been near us, but in an elevated position. He might have stood within our reach, but by the evidence of His greatness, His power and the insignia of His authority been separated from us by an impassable gulf. But here He is, the King of heaven and earth; His throne overtopping all thrones; His dominion embracing all heavens, all earths, all suns, standing on our doorstep.

We have, by courtesy and gracious condescension, sometimes been called into the presence of great dignitaries, but the trappings of their greatness have made a gap between us we could not pass. We have felt awkward and embarrassed in their presence. Their whole attitude and appearance remind us all the time of their vast superiority.

But not so with this Christ. He steps down to our platform. He has taken our form upon Him. He is dressed in our garments. His hands are gnarled and knotted by our tools of labor, His feet bruised upon our stony steps, His face saddened by our sorrows, His body wearied by our toils. He stands upon our level!

Christ stepped down to the level of those around Him when He was upon earth--to the level of all fishermen when He sat eating His bread on the ropes and rigging at the back of Peter's boat; to the varying levels of the multitude when He sat at the great picnic and divided bread which blossomed into greater and greater loaves; when He asked the woman at the well to give Him to drink and put His divine lips to her crude goblet. So He waits at the door to put His lips to the cup of your distresses, your griefs and your tears.

O ye of the poor man's lot! Ye who carry the hod of bricks up the ladder on the wall; ye who ring the pickax down in the gold shaft; ye who have felt the smite of the tempest at mast-head; ye who stand amid the flying spindles and straining straps of the great factory; ye who have sinned and in sinning have broken hope and heart and home and faith and prospects; ye mothers whose little children go to school without any breakfast, despite the ceaseless plying of your needle and thread; ye who sit in the rear tenement basement overworked, overtaxed, overtroubled; I point you to the Christ of the doorstep! He stands upon your dilapidated threshold, knocking, knocking at the shabby door. Let Him in! He will take the bitter out of the cup.

But perhaps the sweetest thought in this text is that if we will but open the door Christ will come in and sup with us.

I see in this intimate touch the great principle of equality and fraternity. Surely this doorstep, sitting-down-at-the-table Christianity is world-wide democracy. While authority will ever, and must necessarily ever, have its place, and God has willed that there shall be leaders, and masters and superiors in every sphere, yet this Christ of Peter's boat and the Samarian well and the cottage tea-table made the scepter and the shovel brothers.

Bring All Men Together

Tapestry and lace must not despise calicoes. Epaulette has no right to be unmindful of blacksmith's apron. Fricasseed fowl should not speak disparagingly of plain bread. There is nothing in this Christ of the Doorstep that causes cathedral to look down upon sailors' bethel. The whole gospel teaching is to bring together the hearts of men.

There are those who do not like the idea. They say there are racial differences that stretch a gulf between man and man that can never be bridged; differences that will ever make those of certain isles and certain lands and certain hues of skin less worthy than others. But Paul knocks that theory down when, standing in the presence of one of the most wealthy and learned audiences of the world, he proclaims in the name of God this democratic doctrine! "God hath made of one blood all nations of men." They started from one Eden, they fell in one transgression, the redeemed are saved by the one and only source of Divine Grace, and are to dwell forever in the one eternal home.

But you must let Him in, you must open the door. Christ will not force an entrance. No virtue or pardon or grace or peace will come to us by compulsion. We must seek, we must ask, we must open.

The beautiful picture of Christ knocking at the door, painted by W. Holman Hunt, was first refused exhibition by the art critics for the reason that the artist had not made any provision for the door to be opened on the outside. When asked for the reason he said: "The conception is figurative of Christ pleading for an entrance at the door of the heart, and the human heart cannot be opened from the outside." Many a lad would have won his lassie if he could have opened the door of her heart. But only we ourselves can open our hearts. Oh, how dreadful, how appalling to have this all-helping, loving Christ so near and yet so far! Upon the threshold, but the door closed!

Kept His Heart's Door Barred

When one of my officers said to a dying, suffering old man this summer, "Christ will help you," he replied: "Well, He never has. Christ has never done anything for me." No; because, although with a sister a Salvationist, a good, loving wife, and Christ on his doorstep through seventy years, he had kept the door of his heart bolted and barred against Him.

A few days ago a lady told me: "I found no comfort in Jesus when my two babies died of pneumonia." No! Because, although Christ had been patiently knocking since she was a little child, she had kept the door closed.

Some people keep Christ out because they are ashamed of the condition of their souls. They intend one day to open unto Him, when they have put out of their lives evil, foul practices. A man said to me during the camp meetings at Old Orchard: "How can I sing hymns, mingle with the good or pray, with my wicked life? I must prepare myself to be a Christian."

No! Do not wait to make preparation. Sometimes, when a child or a mother is sick, the wife of the one rich man of the village will visit a poor home. As soon as word is received, oh, what a scurrying and scampering around in a pitiful attempt to improve appearances! The one clean cloth is spread to hide the scars and stains of the old rickety table; a mat, little more than a rag, is laid over the filthiest part of the floor; a clean pinafore covers the dirty, threadbare dress of the little girl. And the squalid, foul condition of the room is somewhat covered. But not so

9

with this Christ of the doorstep! He would rather see us as we are!

He will cleanse the room Himself. He says so. "I will sprinkle clean water upon you, and ye shall be clean," is God's way. And does not the Apostle Paul say of the man in Christ: "Old things are passed away; behold, all things are become new!"

Let Him in! Let Him in!

The State of Indiana is called the "Hoosier State." This is because the early settlers were afraid to have door-knobs or any kind of a latch that could be opened from the outside lest their enemies should surprise them. And so when there was a knock at the door they would cry out: "Who's here?"

It is not without purpose that there is no means of opening the door of our hearts from the outside. The enemies of our souls are ever cunningly trying to gain admittance. We cannot afford to open to every knock, and so, like the wary settlers of old, we find it wise to cry, "Who's here?" Sweeter than the chimes that ring over the hills of paradise is the answer: "It is I, be not afraid--I, the Prince of Peace, the Babe of Bethlehem, the Christ of God!"

10

Last Opportunity for Repentance

Oh, ye who are sitting by a desolated hearth; ye who are wrestling with suffering and trials; ye who know not which way to turn for trouble; ye who are burdened with sin, arise and fling wide the door! The Judgment is coming, eternity is coming; this very hour may be your last opportunity for repentance. The heart of the Eternal God yearns for you. He has been knocking many a long day at the door of your soul.

When the baby died He knocked; when you lay in the hospital He knocked; through every sunny day and every stormy night, and every harvest gathering and every Spring morning, and every Autumnal withering, He knocked and knocked and knocked.

Hear Him and let Him into your heart. He waited for you all last year, and all the year before and all your life. He has waited for you with blood on His brow and tears in His eyes, and two outstretched mangled hands of love, knocking, knocking, knocking!

Oh, let Him in! He will bring comfort dearer than can be found in a mother's arms. As in the midnight sky of Bethlehem, He will break through your darkest night with angelic song; He will bring pardon. Under the first step of His feet sins of a lifetime will perish. Remember, He made a palace of a stable because the door was open to Him. He passed the inn by because the door was closed.

Your whole life will be a laughing, praising, gladdening experience if you let Him in. Blessed be God for this unspeakable gift of this Christ of the Doorstep!

11

Christ as a Mother

As one whom his mother comforteth, so will I comfort you (Isaiah 66:13).

From The War Cry (New York), May 13, 1916.

Yes, I have written of "Christ the Pilot," navigating our barque through the voyage of life, for life is no calm lake, canopied with blue skies, but a great, dangerous sea, billowed up with trouble and overhung with storm clouds threatening disaster.

I have written of "Christ the Shepherd," with weary, bleeding feet, and torn, patient hands, scaling highest steeps and penetrating deepest chasms, looking for the one lost lamb, although ninety-nine were safe in the fold, for "all we like sheep have gone astray."

I have written of "Christ the Gardener," standing in our midst as one of life's humblest workmen, a most practical Savior, with understanding sympathy entering into close bonds with all the toilers of the world, for how apt we are to break down under our labors, as well as depart from a just and true course in our business without Jesus.

I have written of "Christ the Friend," standing close up to our hearts, making joy the more joyous, sorrow bearable and burdens easy, for every heart at some time knows the vicissitudes of exquisite emotion, and into each life "some rain must fall."

I have written of "Christ the Light," rivalling all suns and paling all earthly brilliance, making plain the traveler's path, shedding a gleam into the mariner's midnight and throwing across the "valley of the shadow" a shaft of resurrection light, because for all, one by one, earth's lightships sink, and without Him we find ourselves groping like the Egyptians of old in the horror of a great darkness; and I have written of "Christ the Song," "Christ the Everlasting," "Christ the Wonderful," "Christ the Father," and many others.

But here I am attempting to write of Christ as a mother, and at the onset my mind is flooded with overwhelming suggestion.

All portrayals of Christ are wonderful, but as we stand spellbound before a masterwork, so our very hearts are held in wonder as we look upon this picture, which, in its intimate human revelation of matchless love divine, captivates and conquers as beyond and over all.

There are one or two characteristics surrounding motherhood which, in all reverence, I would suggest as a worthy similitude of Christ.

Mother's Preference

In the best, happiest and most carefully regulated families there are favorites. It may be concealed, never admitted, fought against, but no matter, there it is. There are those among the children--that boy or that girl--to whom father's and mother's heart goes out with something special in their affection. With father it is generally for his son--usually the firstborn. What high hopes are flung over that little head brimming full of mischief! Father says,

13

"That's a fine, bright boy. He will take my place in the business one day. He will perpetuate my name. He shall not be handicapped by lack of education as I was. Never mind if I have to toil and sacrifice to send him to college-- he's worth it. He is a great boy, that boy."

But how different with mother. Her favorite is the delicate one. She who can never bear what the others can or do what the others do; she who has the awful setback of a crooked spine or blind eyes or a defective heart. It is she for whom mother makes her greatest sacrifices; it is she for whom mother stays home to make happy when the rest have gone to the party or the circus; it is she for whom mother puts aside the most dainty portion of the meal; it is this little, pale face mother kisses the oftenest; this little frail form which she carries in her arms the most tenderly.

Yes, the little hunchback or the little lad whose mind is defective or the one who will have to go all through life on crutches is mother's favorite.

As a mother, our natural weaknesses and finite setbacks only draw out His great heart the more toward us. This must be the explanation of how exceptionally happy and joyous we so often find those who are sorely afflicted.

The sick room of dear Ensign May Rogers--although she has been bedridden for eighteen years and unable to move any part of her suffering body for eleven years--had such a supernatural sunshine in it that as soon as I was in her presence I knew it to be the audience-chamber of the King of kings.

Oh, take courage and comfort, you who feel yourselves so weak and wanting! Remember, that not only is it written, "a bruised reed shall He not break," but that your very afflictions and frailties will the more endear you to His heart. Service rendered to Him despite your natural handicap is of so much greater worth than service rendered out of every advantage, and if in your voyage toward the blest shore you are beset with human disadvantages, remember, as a mother, He careth for you the more.

Mother's Understanding

With a mother the child's small grievances and distresses are large. The broken toy or the cut finger or the bumped head may not be much to father. He is sorry to see the little one cry, but is so engaged with life's sterner matters that he cannot attach any importance to such infinitesimals. He says, "Oh, that's nothing; it will soon be better; run along!"

But mother gauges the significance of the grievance by the extent of the sorrow caused the child and seeks to repair the break, no matter what it may be or bind up the wound or try her best to make less the disappointment. Just as big as the trouble is to the little one, or the young boy, her understanding sympathy makes it big to her.

And it is just this that makes us even now--long years after her sweet presence has passed beyond our reach--in our hearts tell her our troubles still, for she always understood what our troubles were to us and, although we are children of much older growth, we have never found anyone else who understands quite as she did. She would always bid us tell her all, saying, "No matter how great the mistake you have made or how disastrous the position in which you find yourself or how stupidly or wrongly you have acted, tell me all how it happened;" and we would know as we looked into the anxious, tender eyes that we could depend upon the last drop of blood in the precious form to help us.

As a mother. Is this not what it means--"Come, let us reason together?" "Whatever the nature of your sins tell Me about them, and though they be red like crimson they shall be as wool. Whatever the character of your sorrows, tell Me about them, and 'as one whom his mother comforteth so will I comfort you.'" Is this not what it means--He is "acquainted with grief?" All grief, every grief, and that in His limitless knowledge and boundless kindness He persuades us to turn to Him and tell Him all our sorrows, our mistakes, our sins, and He will listen. He will understand, He will forgive, He will cleanse, He will dry our tears, and with that kiss which rivals every embrace known to men and gods He will seal us His.

Mother's Patience

Of all vocations motherhood brings the greatest strain upon human forbearance. Mother's nerves may be taxed by scrubbing floors and mending clothes by day and watching the sick infant by night, yet rarely does she give evidence that her endurance is breaking, rather throughout her great profession, with all its branches of tending and training, she shows that her patience grows but stronger with trial.

This is the reason there is no teacher like mother. Life's earliest lessons require such exceptional patience. It takes mother to teach the alphabet. Who without chiding or irritation would go over and over so many times the difference between M and N, and B and R?

Much has been written to extol and explain the wonders of Froebel and Montessori to the infant understanding, but how far short they fall of the ingenuity of mother! Countless means and measures suggest themselves to her mind whereby the difficult becomes easy and the seemingly unexplainable comprehensible. Look, for instance, at the clever and often amusing inventions by which she aids the child to grasp the multiplication table--sometimes by the use of apples, sometimes beads, sometimes bricks, inventions and plans which she only could devise.

Looking back to my own childhood I seem to see my mother as if it were but yesterday, with her loving, gentle face and soft, wondrous eyes, leaning over me at the piano. So simple and so plain she made these first sheets of music, with all the printed notes looking like a lot of fork-prongs engaged in pugilistic combat. I see now the delicate hand upon the key-board, showing me over and over again the same exercise, note by note, without one impatient utterance, or one word as to my being slow or stupid, which would have so disheartened me.

Ah! Mothers are wonderful, and in nothing more wonderful than in their patience with their children.

As a mother. Our stupidity and slowness cannot tire Him out, and He never expects from us clearer vision or quicker understanding or more efficient service than is ours to give. He leads us, step by step, note by note, letter by letter. He does not crowd all our lessons upon us at once; does not ask all our sacrifices the same day. He measures

17

out the exact weight of the burden for His children and then gives strength accordingly. He is willing to wait for our souls to "grow in grace." I believe this is the chief reason why His abundant mercy has veiled from our eyes the future, for what could more greatly intensify the acuteness of today's sorrows than a knowledge of tomorrow's?

Oh, the ineffable wisdom and incomparable tenderness of Christ's school! He stoops down to our infantile minds and teaches us "line upon line, precept upon precept;" one day this, another day that. He has been teaching some of us thirty and some of us fifty years the same lesson, from the same book, and we do not properly know it yet, and yet it is so simple. Thousands of times He has explained it to us in different ways--that one little word of five letters-- T-R-U-S-T. We still stumble over it, yet God's patience is not exhausted.

If He had been as a schoolmaster He would have punished us; if as a father He would have been angry with us, but He is as a mother, and so He bears with us and leads us on, little by little, into a perfect knowledge of a perfect trust in Him, which makes life and death an unbroken morning.

Mother's Forgiveness

In this mother's heart is enthroned, above every other value, forgiveness, for in her tremendous and boundless capacity to forgive she outstrips everything else that is human and comes closer to the Divine.

Look at her pardoning love following that wayward boy. With his broken promises piled like burned-out cinders in her heart; with her repeated expectations raised by his resolutions earthquaked into heaps of ruin; with all the flowering of his promising manhood blighted ere it bloomed before her hopeful gaze; with all the ruins of his early wreck staring her in the face, yet that undying, tenacious, immortal something, which alone finds life in the breast of mothers, rises up and refuses to abandon him--to let him go--to declare him hopeless, but again and again, and for the seventy-seventh time will hope, will forgive, will trust, will have bright visions, will pray, will believe, will expect, although probabilities declare to her that she is only lengthening out the long suffering path for her poor feet to tread.

When does a mother give a boy up? Where is the milestone that marks the end of the travel of a mother's heart after him? No! Away on highest hill, down in deepest sea, across widest range, she is before him.

I see that poor, wandering son crossing the seas and putting half the world between him and the one who gave him birth, but he cannot get away from mother's heart. I see him flinging the last remnants of respectability behind him in a deeper plunge into infamy and crime, but his mother's heart goes down with him into the darkness.

I see his waywardness turning from him every other well-wisher, every other helper, every other friend, but his mother's heart is closer yet, and no matter how branded and sin-stained he comes back to her he will find her waiting with her wounded breast ready for him to lean his poor bruised head upon, and her arms outstretched to gather him into love and pardon.

As a mother, God is slow to give a man up. He gives the wanderer chance after chance to prove His promise to pardon and to save.

Walk through the dismal corridors of our penal institutions, look into the faces of those who haunt the underworld, and tell me if anything else but Divine love can account for the very existence of these forlorn hopes. They have been given up by society, given up by their friends, given up by their families, given up by their own despairing souls; but all their wickedness and abominations have not carried them out of the reach of Christ's pardoning forgiveness. He has not given them up. He still puts opportunities in their way. He still makes mercy's call to ring in their ears. He still sends rays of light to illumine their souls' midnight.

A human savior said to me, "That man is irreclaimable; words are wasted on him; effort thrown away."

"Well," I replied, "Christ has not given him up; He still sees something in him to pity, something deep under all the chaos to which to appeal; something--oh, miracle of compassion--something He died to redeem!"

Who can measure the range of such pardon? Who can sound the depths of such mercy? Have you who read this forgotten it? Did you say, "I have sinned away my day of grace; I have lost all claim upon the One who died for me?" Do you say, "I am lost?" No, not lost, not beyond help! You will be if you go on--yes, by the unalterable and ineffable laws of judgment--you will be lost if you go on, but not lost yet, for God has not given you up.

His nail-pierced hands are outflung to meet you, and his hand is As a mother's hand. What it touches, it heals. It is not a sheriff's hand, this hand which would take hold of you. Not a hard hand, a cold hand, an enemy's hand. It is a gentle hand, a soft hand, a sympathetic hand--even as a mother's. There is no one like mother can put a child to sleep.

When the party is over, and the games are done and the guests are all gone, it is no easy work to get the child to sleep, and as soon as nurse or aunty or the big sister ceases to pat the back or take their foot from the rocker, the large eyes open, and the work must be done all over again.

Even father is of no use here, but mother gathers up the little thing and, sitting in the rocking chair, swings back and forth, and there is an opiate in the arms that circle the little body and a sedative in the soothing breast upon which the head is laid and a lullaby as of distant bells in the voice which softly sings, and before the old clock calls out another half hour flown the child is asleep.

As a mother, God has His own way of putting His child to sleep.

We need not fear that dread hour. He will gather us as a mother gathers her child, in His arms everlasting, and upon His breast will hush our weariness into rest perpetual.

I think upon the day my mother died. She passed away in a little cottage by the sea. It was stormy, and the waves, which leapt high against the rugged rocks were so like the sorrow which struck hard against our breaking hearts. We were called to her bedside, and although for two long years we had expected it, it seemed incredible to have to associate her with death. She had been so vital to us, such

21

a forerunner, so triumphant in her individual warfare, so glorious in her self-forgetting service for others. How could we reconcile her splendid powers with the fact of dissolution?

But death was there. We could see its gray shadow upon the precious face. The terrible suffering which had racked her was suddenly allayed, she was restful--quiet. She was beyond all speech. Her eyes, which held the brilliancy of stars to the last, passed from one child to another and then fastened upon my father's face--that face which had been the one face in all the world to her.

It seemed that she had an understanding with my father that if speech left her before death came, and if she realized Christ was with her in the valley, she would wave her handkerchief that she might tell her husband and her children all was well with her at the last. And so rallying her remaining strength she raised it up--up--up, once, twice, thrice. Only an instant it remained uplifted; then the worn, tired arm sank, but still the hand was raised, and when that could no longer be upheld, her thin forefinger moved back and forth, back and forth, then fell, the eyes closed, and she was asleep. But we had the message; we knew that she had found in the valley the One for whom she had looked, and that upon His breast He had given "His beloved sleep."

For all time that precious finger of my dying mother, covered with the little white handkerchief signaling the triumph of grace in death will mean more to my soul's faith than all the theological books and scientific arguments history has ever known.

Thou Shalt Call His Name Jesus

Thou shalt call his name JESUS: for he shall save his people from their sins (Matthew 1:21).

From The War Cry (New York), December 25, 1926.

Much care must be exercised in the interpretation of Shakespeare's immortal question, "What's in a name?" if the answer is to be given with any semblance of discrimination or judgment. A mere negation is certainly not sufficient, for sometimes the whole story is in a name. A man's name becomes so inseparably identified with his life and character that it may be regarded as a sort of miniature biography with the high spots for good or evil starred in the preface. Or it may be likened to a face by which he is unmistakably and universally recognized.

There are names we cannot hear without a shudder; and there are names whose beloved cadences fall on our ears like divinely sacred music and are an inspiration to all men. Among these latter may be mentioned "mother," the sum of all life's blessings; "friend," sweetest flower of altruism; "the baby," which vibrates perhaps the finest and most sensitive chords of the human heart.

Then there are the great names that stand out like mountain peaks in the long history of man.

Moses, for all time, stands for exalted personal integrity, for constructive statesmanship, for legislation founded on the principles of eternity and sublime faith in God. Of David, the sweet singer of Israel, we invariably recall God's

23

declaration that he was a man after His own heart. Paul, to whom was revealed the secret of secrets, the omnipotence of Divine love, is synonymous with Divine revelation. Alexander the Great, with all his glory, portrays the pitiable limitations of mere human ambition. Nero, "one compound of mud and blood" as his people called him, is a synonym for bestial brutality. When we hear such names as Peter the Hermit, Savonarola, Wycliff and Luther, we behold again the undimmed torches of truth with which they defied the darkness of superstition, overcame false doctrine, heresy and schism and blazed a trail throughout the ages for the progress of the Christian faith.

At the name of Washington our pulses leap with enthusiastic patriotism, and before our mental vision there rises the noble form of that "statesman, soldier, patriot, sage, reviser of creeds, teacher of truth and justice, achiever and preserver of liberty; the first of men, founder and savior of his country, father of his people, solitary and unapproachable in his grandeur." The name of Abraham Lincoln will ever stand for the two greatest forces of national life--liberty and union. Such a name as Frances Willard compels us to bow in reverence and admiration for the intellectual breadth and spiritual powers of her sex, and in the realization of her message her memory will ever be monumental in the homes of America. Who can hear the name of William Booth, Founder of The Salvation Army, and not remember the man, the life, the service to the world, of the "Apostle of the Poor?"

But there is one name transcendently unique in the wealth of its suggestion and meaning. A name presaged before birth and heralded above all others; a name that

24

made heaven and earth to stand in inexpressible and mysterious wonderment while angelic choirs proclaimed its natal morn. A name that flashed in the meteor that swung over Bethlehem hills, and led the Magi of the East to cross the desert trails that they might behold Him. A name that pierced the hard nature of Herod and convulsed his throne with fear. A name despised by the Pharisaical magnates of Jerusalem, but crowned by the lowly fishermen of Galilee as the Promised of the Lord Most High.

Wherever this name has traveled it has abolished the inhuman practices of heathen worship. It has broken the cords that bound the girl-widow to the funeral pyre. It has delivered little children from yawning-mouthed crocodiles. It has penetrated the black pall of superstition and swept the midnight sky of heathendom with a blaze which all the powers of sin and hell can never extinguish.

And by what reason have such signs followed the progress of this name in its starlike course through the ages? The answer is writ in the language of heaven, in the fulfillment of prophecy. It is the name of the Only Begotten of the Father, the supreme expression of the divine will for man's everlasting destiny--in all ages, for all colors and all creeds. And just as the rays of the sun, in innumerable billions, come millions of miles in night-dispelling energy till not a vestige of darkness is left to mar the splendor of its meridian glory, so this name of Jesus will dispel all darkness from the souls and lives of men.

"Thou shalt call his name Jesus: for he shall save his people from their sins" (Matthew 1:21).

"Thou," addressed to Joseph: thus the divine purpose imposes human obligation. This is God's way, God's law, from the beginning. "Shalt"--it appears to me that this *shalt* is an imperative assertion made by Jehovah, and that it is a very serious matter to interfere with it. There was no alternative, no need for family discussion, no other name preceding and no other name following. Through all the realms of Glory, through all the caverns of the lost, through the length and breadth of earth, His name forevermore is Jesus! That *shalt* of Almighty God remains for all time.

"Call"--tell it out, proclaim it from Zion's hill in the valley of Jehoshaphat, on Mount Olivet, in the Temple of Diana, in the slave marts of Europe, in the black holes of heathendom, in the royal corridors of kings and emperors, in the lowest regions of the wretched; wherever men huddle together in misery and sin, tell it out.

"His name"--it is His own name; it defines His personality; it proclaims His infinity; it declares His divinity. It is the name by which we shall ever honor His birth, life, death, resurrection and mediatory place at the Throne of the Father in the skies--JESUS!

But the question is not yet fully answered. There is a miraculous, dawn-breaking, sin-pardoning and wound-healing reason; the whole world stood still and the angels flung down light over the midnight hills while heavenly choirs announced it; it was in the "glory to God," in the "peace on earth," in the "good will to men." "Thou shalt call his name Jesus: for he shall save his people from their sins."

I like the personal objective in the coming of our Lord--His people. There is the ring of patriotism in it. There is the admission of the greatest sorrow that ever shadowed the face of Him that sitteth on the Throne in it. God wanted a people for His own, His very own, when the world was still in its cradle. He gave lands and herds and silver and gold and cities and palaces and princes and rulers to the people He had chosen; but, with pathos it is recorded, "He came unto his own, and his own received him not!" We know how they despised His marvelous gifts, how they forsook the unseen for the seen, how they treated His prophets with disdain, how they journeyed to the groves of the Philistines, how they substituted an earthly throne for the glory of the Shekinah, and finally, having lapsed into civil belligerency, how they were destroyed by their enemies, shattered and scattered throughout the world.

Mother, father, can you imagine what would be your feelings if not one, but all of your children grew up to curse you, forsook the paths of their childhood, and "turned every one to their own way?" And if you saw the whole world in similar rebellion would you not first, out of them all, if it were possible, select your own for succor and salvation? And with what infinitely more love and compassion God looked upon the backsliding of Israel! Consequently, the very first note of deliverance, echoing and re-echoing through the galleries of heaven and vibrating through every artery of earth, offered salvation to His people. I am one of those who believe that the time will come when our Savior "shall see of the travail of his soul and be satisfied."

Nevertheless, the reason for Jesus' coming was universal and all-comprehensive. "God so loved the world that he gave his only begotten Son, that whosoever

27

believeth in him should not perish, but have everlasting life." He came to bring salvation to all peoples.

What is wrong with the world? It is not lack of bread. It is not the wrath of man against man, nation against nation. There is a sense in which that evil cures itself. The big gaps in national and international strife have become wider and wider as time has gone on. War is spasmodic. Men cannot always be fighting.

Neither is that which is wrong with the world a lack of law and order. Regrettable as disorder is, it is not so rampant today as it has been in the history of peoples centuries gone by. One of the wonders of our time is the peaceable and orderly life of the millions of people in our great cities. No, run up the gamut of our civilization's activities and you cannot ascribe the cause of the world's unrest to any specific ill--economic, social or commercial. The world's chief need is still to be found in the human heart.

The densely materialized brains of Judea would have hailed even the Nazarene had He proclaimed the overthrow of the Romans and the restoration of the Kingdom of Israel. But what permanent good would a material kingdom have been in overcoming a spiritual Caesar? The empire to be overthrown was in possession of the human will. Hence the Lord's cry, "Thy kingdom come!" Unseen, but almighty; set not in wealth or material power, but love; enthroned, a kingdom from everlasting to everlasting, with God as King.

Jesus is the name above all others, because He saves from sin. He goes to the root of all evil, all tyranny, all disorder--sin. He has conquered this imperious monster that wrecks humanity, and He ever lives to realize in every surrendered life the glory of the triumph. The venom of the sting He entirely extracts, the leprous disease He completely cures. The Saviorhood of Jesus is sufficient.

Jesus is the name above all others because He made Himself partner with us in our sufferings, He "tasted death for every man." Few kings know their kingdoms, fewer still their subjects. But Jesus knows us all. He knows us not only as a people, a nation, a church, a society; He knows us individually. He knows our weaknesses, our temptations, our trials, our fears, our failures, our physical ailments, our mental doubts, our shipwrecked hopes, for "even the very hairs of your head are all numbered." This we have upon His own word: and Paul says also that He is not one who "cannot be touched with the feeling of our infirmities, but was in all points tempted like as we are, yet without sin."

Jesus is the name above all others because it promises most for the world. He is the Executive of heaven and earth. He is the Dispenser of the gifts and graces of the Comforter; He bestows the Holy Spirit. His promises anticipate every need. If a deliverer arose in London tomorrow promising work for England's unemployed, he would be proclaimed greater than all the monarchs that have been crowned in Westminster Abbey. But here is Jesus, King of kings and Lord of lords, whose power enables us to overcome all evil. In His hands we become the subjects of a science that turns the bitter into sweet, the evil into good and death into the messenger of life.

Jesus is our mediator. The short span of His life on earth, from the manger to the cross, has forged an inseverable link between man and God. With one hand He takes hold on omnipotence, and with the other He lifts up frail and broken humanity. By His divinity He is God's Son; by His humanity He is our Elder Brother. He will safeguard all the claims of God, for He has filial relationship with Him. He will have understanding sympathy with us, for He "is acquainted with our griefs." Heaven charged Him with its momentous, unparalleled mission, but He never lost sight of our interests, and to save our souls from death He flung His broken body across the yawning gap of our destruction. Through Him we know the Divine mind and understand the glory of our destiny. Why then should I hesitate to lay all life's cares and mistakes and sins and troubles at His feet?

Jesus is the name above all others because it saves from sin. The Magdalene fell at His feet in humble contrition and love. The woman of Samaria ran all excited to the men of the city, saying: "Come, see a man, which told me all things that ever I did: is not this the Christ?" He is the sinner's Savior. He has the knowledge, the power and the passion of a Savior. He understands sin, its awfulness, its peril and its pain. Men catalogue and condemn the enormity of the act; Jesus takes into account the strength of the tempter, and comes with power to save the soul which left to itself is inevitably lost. I call upon all the saints on earth and all the redeemed in heaven to lift with me hallelujahs! Ten thousand hallelujahs!

The Bible records that an angel one day measured heaven. I can see that rod jeweled in the sun that never grows old. All along the golden highways he measured, all along the sea of glass, all along the walls of jasper--from portal to portal--hundreds of miles around, as the Bible estimates. Although the account be figurative, what a wonderful home it is that Jesus is preparing for us. And it is a better heaven now than when John wrote of it. A multitude of the redeemed have passed in since then. My mother is there! My father is there! Your loved ones are there. But, best of all, Jesus is there! We shall sit down by the waters of the river of life, o'erhung by the tree bearing twelve manner of fruit, the leaves of which tree are for the healing of the nations. We shall not want for anything all through eternity. No suffering will draw the features, no discord will jar the ear, no fears will grip the heart, no tears will blind the eyes. *Jesus will be there!* Always there. *Eternal summer*--eternal joy--eternal love.

Jesus is the name above all others because it is the stupendous, incontrovertible, superlative fact of the universe.

We migrate today from the shores of the Stars and Stripes, and following the star set in the heaven of His will, we find again the Babe in the Manger. Blessed, holy Babe! We kneel by the crude grass basket that lies in the feeding bin and behold in the brow of Mary's Child the glory of our King; no, sweeter far, we read the Promise of God--the Bread of Heaven--Jesus our Savior, our Pardon-bringer, our Redeemer and Friend! We return to this land of liberty, this glorious diamond of jeweled States, and look out the mangers where lie the poor and the outcast, the sick and the suffering. We kneel by their cots and upon their foreheads we trace the reflection of Bethlehem's glory--Jesus, the world's Redeemer!

This is the work of The Salvation Army in the United States of America. It was for this high office I was commissioned "The Commander," the title by which I am known as the leader of our organized forces. But at this kindly season, Christmas, which brings human affection to its highest tide, my heart abounds with good will and the spirit of oneness with all men. Let me not then upon this day, when all minds are upon Bethlehem's manger, be thought of as *The Commander*, but as one equal with my people in the divine bonds of loving fellowship and service made possible by the newborn King. If God so loved us, let us so love one another.

Chapter Two
Children and Young People

Tender Flocks

From The War Cry (Toronto) in two parts: February 11 and 18, 1899.

"The children are tender." Children! The very word is tender-- tenderly precious: so bewitching in its attraction as to rival the whole of the vocabulary world. The letters forming it shine in the mind of almost every man as linked stars interwoven with fairy memories of some little being that has helped to compose its vast crowd.

Childhood's merriment has been the music which has vibrated through ten thousand halls, waking by its infectious charm echoes of sweetest strain in the older hearts; their little faces, the bloom, casting sweetest perfume through the humblest walk, making a very garden of fragrance to even the poorest dwelling. In the prattle of their tongues and the patter of their feet, a million mothers have heard the tramp of whole regiments of promise as to what the future will bring.

Half the toil of the world is for the children; half its sufferings gladly borne for their sake. Who could give the number of mothers who would lie down and die were it not for baby?

I know that some men's humanity is so mutilated and slaughtered by sin and shame as to forget their parental duty to helpless infancy--but oh! The countless fathers who, every time they thrust the spade in, do so in the interests of the children. They are the pride of ten million hearts. They are the light of ten million homes. They are the hope of ten million futures. Take them out of the streets and those streets are damper, colder and rougher. Take them out of the most poverty-stricken hovels, and such are darker, bleaker and poorer. Take them away from the lonely and destitute, and desolation is complete. A working woman said to me only last week, as I patted the cheek of a little fellow of six years, "Ah! his father's sun rises and sets in those two eyes!" And so it is with numerous homes: all their light shines through the two windows found in a little face.

No! this world of ours could not get on without them. It would be too empty, and, if mortality statistics speak truly, when they average so large a percentage of deaths under seven, then the greater part of heaven's population is made up of the half unfolded flowerettes of earth's tearful gardens.

Oh! Jerusalem the golden!
There all our birds that flew
Our flowers half unfolden
Our pearls that turned to dew.

Then it is their tenderness that constitutes their influence. They are a continual proof of "gentleness hath made me great." Will eternal records reveal all the miracles wrought by these small travelers on life's paths? What chains of inseverable bond, even fastening love on earth to love in heaven, have been linked by infant fingers? What numerous gulfs, dark, deep and bitter, have been bridged but by a baby's form? What walls of adamantine have been lifted, withstanding the buffeting of all time, by a child's weak arms?

A day or two back I stepped into a tastefully arranged studio. There stood, in the softened light of a shaded lamp, the tall, dark figure of a man, whose countenance, by its massive outlines and compression of feature, depicted a nature of exceptional strength, perhaps determined to severity. Fearlessly upon his shoulder nestled a babe of some two years; it rested its waxen cheek against the swarthy complexion of the father like a birdling lighting amidst the shady foliage of spreading oak or a pink bud sleeping on a leafy spray.

Knowing the man as extremely sparing in expressions of sympathy or affection, I watched with some interest the varying lights which flickered across the face, as with tenderest word and touch he fondled the little mite. I said in my heart that surely God has sent these little starlings as messengers from the sky to thrust back the flood-gates which would lock the deeper waters of man's better self, and by appealing gentleness prevent many an austere spirit hardening into stone. Looking upon the strong contrast drawn between a nature which is the embodiment of mental and physical force and the infant innocence of the clinging child, I realized how all its power to appeal to the best and highest side of this character was found in the very truth of which my verse speaks that "the children are tender."

By reason of this tenderness they have blessed the most despicable characters, in awakening a chivalry which has sought to undertake for their frailty in protecting, nursing and guiding them, for it is in this tenderness that lies their unspeakable worth, which declares that any effort thrown

36

into their reaching and saving is fraught with inestimable import.

No wonder Jesus lifted that pyramid running higher than synagogue, creed, belief or doctrine, and upon its pinnacle, reaching heaven's own land, placed a figure--small in stature--and said, "Of such is the kingdom of heaven."

Again, They are Tender in Years

The broader ways of sin's rude and thorny paths are untrodden by innocent's feet. Although some are cradled in most unfavorable circumstances, the mind in youth remains largely ignorant of the cunning devices of heavy sins. Of a multitude of those crimes which rob man of his self-respect, blast and damn his career, children are ignorant.

Tens of thousands, especially in this country, have never known how it felt to be drunk and have looked upon the idiotic demeanor of an intoxicated man with as much wonder as horror. Thousands have never found how successfully fraud and deception can be practiced, making a man a wretch in time, and a lost soul in eternity, and, to say the least, consider what falsehoods they may resort to in a most condemned and risky business. The life of the street lamp, with its burning allurements they are totally ignorant of; they have neither tasted its fascination or known its burden. Fashion and worldliness have but besprinkled their young hearts with the spray of their waters, awakening in some early germs of pride, yet so far are they from the depths of these infatuations, that they care little as to what they look like and nothing as to what they are thought of.

Full of Intrinsic Worth are These Tender Years

We cannot exaggerate their value. The importance of our chance with the children is magnified more by reason of what they are not than by what they are; by what they know not than by what they know. Their very restless and undecided state of mind and heart, which often lays such fierce claim upon our patience, is our opportunity. They are like an unplanted garden, the production of whose soil is solely at the skill of the cultivator; you can make them to spring in briar or bloom in myrtle. The years of youth are our chance.

With the diseases that attack the fold, it is an easy matter to rectify in the lamb what becomes a difficult and often impossible undertaking in the old sheep. Nature's accidents in twisted branch and dwarfed plant, and creatures' misfortunes in distorted frame and crooked limb, would all say childhood is the time to train the vine, make the character, to rectify failings and save the soul. Wait not till the rough impress of sinning years have left their deadly stamp upon the disposition, robbing even from God His chance in handing over to Him not the best, but marred and spoiled material.

Then, the Children are Tender in Conscience

All the combined plannings and schemings of hell are for the complete annihilation of the conscience God has given to every man; this once destroyed, then the soul inevitably drifts and sinks. This magnetic needle which points through the midnights and cyclones of life unerringly to the eternal harbors of heaven--this God-stationed force--martialled in the human breast to fight to the last in the interests of the soul, this victor which by its ceaseless struggling has saved countless numbers from the doom of the damned--would have led, and will yet lead, all men up, eternally up, if yielded to and its dictates followed. But conscience refuted, sin stamps out its susceptibility, leaving God and the good but a poor dormant agency to appeal to.

Oh, conscience!
A boat at midnight sent alone,
To drift upon the moonless sea:
A lute whose leading chord is gone;
A wounded bird that hath but one
Imperfect wing to soar upon,
Are like what I am without thee.

In our day I often think some men have no conscience. Like the animal, so wrapped up in the present do they live, as though today embraced all, ignoring an eternal beyond.

But the children--they are very tender. It is not so very long since God sent them to bless the world with that keen perception of right and wrong, which, with its strong

39

tendency toward virtue and blushing aversion to guilt, would put many a man of mature years to shame.

In the child there lives, strong, healthy and bright, what man has abused and slain. It is there to respond *yea* and *amen* to all condemnation of evil and all upholding of truth. With very few exceptions, no matter how depraved the boy, if you tell him that lying is wicked, cruel and bad, all that is in him will rise up in defense of the statement, and you may be sure that his conscience is beside you, sentencing the evil in even blacker terms.

Through my active life, I have had varied experience with children and have often been impressed by the way they sought me out after public meetings conducted in simplicity exclusively for their benefit. Even those known as the most wayward have with sobs, or with attitude of great confusion, tumbled out their confessions of stolen jam, fights at school and other sins. Trivial they would seem, if any sin with its momentous capacity to spread can be trivial, but manifesting the readiness of the young soul to turn Godward and flee the snares, perils and disasters of the downward track. While the conscience condemns stealing of jam or fighting at school, it is our day for using it to bar the doors of the soul against all evil.

The Children are Tender in Spirit!

Is not this the pearl they carry that makes them so irresistibly attractive, and dear to almost every heart? They are like the brook: their most stormy outbursts are only ruffled riplets consequent to passing breezes: if they are quickly angered they quickly forgive. To carry a grudge or nurse a jealousy is foreign to a child. If they are crushed, they quickly forget, with a sweet oblivion which would have taken the bitterness out of many an adult's life. They quickly cry, they are quickly sorry, they are quickly led; they are April-like, all smiles and showers, only with the sunshine far exceeding the rain.

Oh, this dear tenderness of spirit! In it is our chance to guide the feet of ten thousand lambs to "the Shepherd of a thousand hills." Let us be quick and eager and hot in our endeavors to gather them before the thick briars of life's sinful thickets have torn and entrapped them.

They tell me that lambs are easily lost. Once out of the fold, they seem to have no idea of retracing their steps. Children are easily lost, too, and may this not be because it is natural to tenderness to lean like the ivy, which wraps its sensitive tendrils around that which is nearest presenting the strongest hold, be the wall a moldering one or not. So the children will cling in their dependent gentleness to the example nearest and strongest, be it for good or evil. Let us rush in between them and decay, and build strong walls for their holding.

The Children are Tender in Vast Possibility

In numberless instances, tenderness bespeaks possibility, as the bud tells of the coming flower, and the springing stream of the tossing torrent. Who can tell, looking upon the cradled babe, what vast issues for good or evil nestle there? What infinite fate may hang upon its soul's awakening? Mothers sway eternal destinies as they rock the cot to slumbering song. Little thought the mother of the infant born in a back room of a German inn, and cradled in the clothes basket, that there sounded in its first cry the first note of that voice which was to awaken all Christendom from the night of Roman Catholicism to the day of Protestantism, or that the name she gave him--Martin Luther--was to be that of the greatest reformer of the world.

Neither did the hard-working woman, lifting in her already overburdened arms the additional care of the foundling brought to her door, dream that she clasped the great Lord Gresham, to whose honor and memory was lifted the magnificent piece of architecture of London's Royal Exchange.

So we cannot tell what future blessings or curses play round our doorsteps; we cannot gauge how far-reaching will be the influence for good or bad of the little beings which run in our streets, and sit in our companies, but we can be sure that if God does spare them they will grow up to either add to the misery of the world or help to transpose its sorrow into joy; grow up to either swell the rushing tide of wrongs against God and man or stand in the ranks of His soldiers for the right. I tell you they will either grow up to go down, cursing the day that gave them birth, into the fires of hell or rise to praise His name in the New Jerusalem.

Because of these possibilities--gems invisibly crowning these little brows--we must put in our claim, our claim for God, and fight desperately for their saving. I would like to repeat that word *desperately*, because no warfare can be too hot or fierce, no conflict too long or strong, that is waged for the saving of the children.

The Children Must be Saved

First, because, as I have already shown, tenderness of childhood is our opportunity for conversion. The door to the soul is easier opened in youth than any other time. Get your hand on the latch before the devil has a chance. Keep them off that tree which gave Eve the ghastly knowledge of evil. My sainted mother used to say, "There is a wonderful advantage in not knowing how."

Then the children must be saved because of their influence on the world both today and tomorrow; their feet are smaller than ours; their more tiny hands can hold better on to buttonholes; their little voices better tell the story of Jesus' tender love, or else it is that the old listen better to it when spoken through hesitating lips. I have known children who, in childhood, God has made the spiritual parents of numbers of the worst of sinners. Ah! but you may argue, some children are more spiritually minded than others. Yes, and so are some grown-up people, but we must get them all for God.

In one of our corps in the north of Scotland, the captain had a hard meeting, and on his return told his wife with some discouragement that they had had no souls that night. He evidently did not think that the miserable little boy of seven years old who had knelt at the penitent-form was worth counting. But that seven year old boy today is one of the most successful evangelists of that country, and has been the means of saving thousands of souls. He never lost the consciousness of God's conquering power from that hour.

Now the question is, how to do it? To start with, we must believe in God's ability to change their hearts and lives. The plan of saving grace is sufficiently perfect as to be as easily grasped by the smallest and weakest mind, as by the most mature and intellectual. You must believe with all your heart and soul and strength that the first and tenderest Blesser of children can save them.

If you doubt the possibility, remember God's power in your own case. Should it fail with one a quarter your size?

We Must Work for Their Salvation

Then, with all the tenderness of parental faithfulness, we must work for their salvation.

Don't look upon it as a small part of your duty. It will last the longest, grow the fastest, spread the widest, be the most productive of anything you are doing. Pray, believe and toil for them.

The renowned patriot, Garibaldi, was one day marching at the head of his army down a defile through the Italian mountains, when the war-like train swept up to the lone figure of a woman, crouching, dejected and weeping, by the roadside. The leader's humane heart inquired the cause of the grief: it was a lamb she had lost, she said; one that was straying solitary somewhere on those very mountains, and which she had sought for, but sought for in vain.

Garibaldi called a halt, and with a quick order, dispersed the troops to hunt for the little wanderer. Later the soldiers returned, saying the search was in vain, upon which information Garibaldi started out himself to hunt the lone mountains.

Early next morning his orderly, alarmed at the stillness which prevailed in the general's tent at a late hour, pushed aside the curtain, to find his esteemed leader lying fast asleep, booted and spurred, as he had flung himself, exhausted after his long night's tramp, while under his martial cloak there nestled, quieted from its bleating, the frail and fleecy little wanderer from the fold. If such a one should be so troubled over a lost lamb, how anxious should we be over the flock for whose folding Christ was slain.

We must be patient. They are tender and cannot be overdriven. This implies that we must be forbearing in our searching for them. The Bible says that if hurried they will die. This means that you must beware of killing in trying to cure. Don't expect short legs to take the strides of long ones, and remember that a good heart does not mean an old head. We must be as forgiving as Jesus and not harder on the children than Christ told us to be with the big grown-up offender who should ask forgiveness seventy times seven.

Then we must not give them up--not by word, thought or action--because they may not reach your full anticipations as quickly as you thought. They cannot run the journey in one day. Time and patience will work wonders.

Lead Them Softly

Reprove them firmly, but gently, not hastily or irritably. Get one of the tears of Christ if you can. There were whole lakes full provided when Jesus wept, and I have known one tear to provide all the dew that was necessary for a whole garden of graces in the heart.

Lastly, make them Salvationists. Inspire them with the spirit of the fight. Tell them of the cleansing, healing, uplifting work being wrought under the flag in every country. Enthuse them with a burning ambition to join the ranks, to stand in the fight and link hands with its victors. The children we need. The children we must get. The children, when we have no foe, will stand before us.

A great general sat in council with three of his chief officers; each expressed his firm belief as to what he felt to be the most-to-be-coveted addition to their present armament. One said, "If we could multiply the contents of our war chest, then no enemy should stand against us." Another declared, "If we could better drill the troops, our country's protection would be invincible." The last expressed, "What an enormous advantage there would be found in more skillful implements of battle!" Then the general, with a keen flash in his sharp, grey eye turned to the three warriors and remarked, "You may gather your money. It will be useful. We need it. You may improve your soldiery. The better they fight the more likely they will be to win. You may invent better weapons. Ours are sadly wanting. But as for me, give me the children, and I will conquer the world."

In this I stand with Napoleon and say, "Give the children to me, and I will do the same."

Daisy

(A child-abuse story that sounds familiar in the 1990s)

From The War Cry (Toronto), January 7, 1899.

Daisy by name, and daisy indeed in form. A daisy in a slum perhaps, but all the same a daisy, despite the pinched features, pale cheek, ragged frock and naked feet. She darts up the rickety stairway of the drunkard's home, and to the pale-faced mother, who plied her needle and thread until the early hours of the morning, holds up a bunch of faded flowers and cries, "Look, mother, now I can sell them for something for you for supper." The little bare head and naked feet stand a long time in the biting wind of the winter's night, but no one buys. At last a well dressed man, to the delight of the child, asks: "And what do you expect to get for that faded nosegay, little one?"

"Whatever you like to give, sir."

The heart of the purchaser, evidently touched by the pitiful, appealing glance of the eyes uplifted, gives ten cents, and a looker-on might have thought that the breath of the night had caught the child for the speed with which she passes down the street. It is the first silver coin the tiny fingers have clasped, and too excited to retain her joy, immediately on reaching the wretched home, calls out as she climbs the rickety stairs:

"Oh, mother, mother, ten cents, a gentleman gave it to me for the flowers. I have sold them. "Look, mother," as she holds up a coin, "all shining."

Unfortunately the father is there, has heard the words "ten cents," demands that the money be given him. The child crouches with horror behind the door of the garret.

"Give me that money," cries the father.

"No! no!" screams the child, "I have got it for mamma. It's to buy her something to eat. I've got it. It's my own, for mamma."

The man, enraged with drunken fury, saying, "I'll teach you to keep money from your father," lifts up his foot--a man's foot with a man's boot on--and kicks the little figure against the opposite wall of the garret, which is splashed with her blood. He snatches the coin from the now unconscious fingers and the monster of brutality stumbles downstairs, heedless of where his heavy boot has fallen, into the nearest saloon. He turns just as the man behind the bar is saying:

"Why, you might have thought the little un had got wings fixed on there and then; she simply flew bare feet too; it 'twern't the flowers, you know; they're no worth," pointing to the faded bunch lying on the bar; "but 'twere just to give her somphin. I tell yer, now, I wish I'd given her more; she looked so pitiful and hungry; too--I believe she said her mother was sick; anyway, I never saw feet run like those little uns; I can't get the sight of her out of me eyes!"

The drunken father stays no longer to hear more of the conversation, but turns conscience-smitten into the street. Just at that moment the throb of an Army drum and the ringing strains of cornets attracts attention. Not knowing whither to go, he follows the procession into the barracks. The meeting goes on; somebody talks to him; somebody prays with him; somebody cries over him; and while they sing:

All the waters of the sea cannot wash my sins away,
But Thy precious blood can do the deed today;
Jesus, Jesus, while all my sins I grieve,
Thou canst receive me and cleanse, I believe.

The man gets soundly converted. He hurries home up the stairs, tells his wife the story. He is never going to drink any more, he says. With tears in the woman's eyes, scarcely knowing whether to believe it, she says, "Hush" and points to the little heap of rags and whiteness on the bed. The only color there is the heavy bloodstains on the brow.

"Oh, my God, have I killed her?" the man gasps.

"No, but you have kicked her eye out."

The marble-like figure stirs. "Oh, is that you, papa? Come here to me, papa. I am not dead, and I'm not sleeping, I have heard all you've said to mamma. Oh, I'm so glad you're made good, papa. I don't mind losing my eye, if you'll only be good and good to mamma. I would lose my two eyes to make you good."

The tall figure of the man went down in a heap at the child's side, and the two little arms blindly feeling, found their way round his neck.

"Papa," she asks, "could you sing one of the hymns they sing where they have those bright meetings?"

"Oh, Daisy, I can't sing. I don't know any good songs. I don't know nothing good yet."

"Well, could you just put your arm round me, papa? You know, like you never did, and hold me up and I will sing." The rough arm, unaccustomed to expressions of affection or tenderness, holds up the little form, and the weak, trembling voice, with many quivers from darts of pain rings through the garret:

There is a better world, they say,
Oh, so bright!
Where sin and woe are done away,
Oh, so bright!
There music fills the balmy air,
And angels with bright wings are there,
And harps of gold, and mansions fair,
Oh, so bright!

An angel, kissing the cheek, bears the little spirit to the land of which the child did speak while the brokenhearted father pours on the face, cold in death, the hot and passionate kisses that should have been given in life. The little darling did give her two eyes and the gift thrust open the flood gates of parental affection and let loose the rivers of redeeming grace.

The Tramp of the Coming Worlds

A pulse-quickening appeal to save the little children.

From The War Cry (Chicago), March 18, 1933.

The world decides today what it shall have and be on the morrow. The nation's greatest men and means are not engaged in accomplishing the triumphs of the moment, but in tutoring conquerors for far higher honors than they themselves can carry, as the gardener's best skill is not concentrated upon the natural blossom, but is given to the nurture of the feeble seedling, promising to beautify a coming summer.

What makes the brave admiral content to leave the fleet in other hands to stay all the time in the training ship at home?

What makes the heroic general deny himself the glory of the front to treat of the ethics of courage in the military school?

What makes the great musician take time from his momentous composition and rapt recital to drudge over the rudiments of his art with unskilled fingers?

What makes the world-famed sculptor lay down his own chisel and superintend the ungainly hewing of a clumsy pupil?

Students: the Hope of Tomorrow

What makes the eloquent divine, whose words sway the souls of multitudes, and whose writings rock the convictions of a whole community, fling the whole force of his genius before a roomful of raw students and an army of notebooks and pencils?

Why, on the stage of time, should so many of the best and ablest be engrossed in these curtained toils? Just because, on some near tomorrow, when their last act is performed, the play must pass into other hands, and to fit such is their work.

Curtained now may seem their labors, but within the arena of the future there line up the naval, military, musical, social, political and religious forces whose nucleus they nurture today.

It is in the clatter of little feet which procession in and out of numerous schools that we hear the tramp of the coming worlds. It is in the ring of voices in park and street we catch the declarations of the rights or wrongs of future nations. In the heated shouts of the playgrounds, over won or defeated games we detect the hurrahs of the armies for God or the hisses of the armies against Him.

Arsenals of the Playground

In the rows of little faces behind amateur desks we see the occupants of our future homes or the terrible spectacles of woe and sin peering through prison grating.

Long years back The Salvation Army has recognized this, and with its philanthropic, redeeming agencies pulsating through every land, it has not been behind in spending its brightest and best to get in readiness reinforcements to fall into line when we wear the white robes instead of the blue and have replaced the cap with the crown.

It is from the arsenals of the playground, the schoolroom and the nursery we can only hope to replenish our resources and march out armies of desperadoes to contend for God and truth, when we ourselves are marshaled above.

Napoleon said, "Give me the children and I will conquer the world."

I say there is no village, town, city or country so dark in sin but that if I could have its children I could win it for Jesus. Oh! have we ever been guilty of thinking that it was only a child--of not much account? That it was a condescension, and perhaps a useless one, to try and do anything for it?

Wrapped in the clay of that child's body there burns a spark of immortality which all the hurricanes of the last day cannot blow out. A child is a little casket of infinite possibilities for light or darkness.

While it is often argued that children's work is the most difficult and intricate that can be undertaken, yet we must not lose sight of the mighty advantages which attend all effort put forth for the salvation of the young, advantages which are inevitably absent in our toil among those of older years.

You can be beforehand with the devil, and it is an immeasurable advantage to be first on the field. Before the fascination of worldliness has stolen the affection, you can point to the attraction of a life lived in the enthusiasm of the cross. Before selfish greed has fastened its claim, you can teach the charm of sacrificing and living for another.

Before that sweet influence so peculiar to childhood is perverted by wickedness and deceit, you can direct its powers for righteousness and truth.

Bulwarks of Warning

Children's ignorance of real guilt and sin offers a thousand facilities for increasing their knowledge of God, and if by building bulwarks of warning about them we can keep them from the knowledge of evil, then we lift a fortress for their soul's protection stronger than the united armies of the whole world could raise.

They are like the vine, with its tender tendrils ready and waiting to be nailed to any wall, and the lambs which can be led down any road.

With the adult there are the questions of the mind to be answered; there are the old habits of thirty or forty years to be shaken off; there is a multitude of former connections to be broken.

It takes a very cyclone of convicting truth to break the hardened heart, while the dropping of one gentle appeal will bring a child to contrition.

Some argue that because of this susceptibility of children, their impulses and resolutions for good are not to be relied upon or even encouraged.

This is as cruel as it is ridiculous.

Because the plant is the easier directed in its earlier awakenings, is it advantageous to leave it to grow in distortion until to correct its misshapen form you must break the stem?

I say if there is a season in the soul's history when it is the more easily influenced for good, and if that period is childhood, then every Christian heart and hand should be outstretched to influence the children for God, so that the little feet may be led into the paths of righteousness, and so prevent their "easy influencing days" being used by the devil to drive them into the rear of the throng which crowds the broad road.

Stirred-up Memories

First impressions are the most lasting. This is especially so when those influenced are for good. The mind, in its wonderful ability to leap through time and space with as great ease and rapidity as the eye can blink, is continually carrying us back to the days of childhood, stirring up memories which give us to realize that the early impressions have never been driven from our soul.

We may have wandered from them, we may have lost their track, we may have abused their blessings, but they remain with us, and all the rough usage the heart may have gone through in its intervening travels has never been able to entirely deafen its ear to the home calls of those first impressions for God and goodness.

They are like the carrier pigeons. No matter how far off they have been driven, they will come home. We find them twenty years after pecking at the gate of our soul. So it is with the nursery and Sunday school days. No child can be taught to pray, love the Bible, fear its God, but what, although we may not see the immediate results, those lamps will cast their light over all the shadows which may follow, and make the strongest claims upon that soul for Heaven.

Among the officers of my own Headquarters Staff there are many who were converted under sixteen years of age.

I, myself, when only a little girl of seven, was led to Him who so graciously said, "Suffer the little children to come unto Me, and forbid them not: for of such is the Kingdom of God."

Caskets of the Fondest Hopes

What is there more precious than a child? They are the instrumentalists upon our hearts' finest strings, and draw from them all the majors and minors of life. It is into their little lives is poured earth's strongest of all loves--a mother's love.

A whole world gives, unconditionally, its compassion and affection to the children. No one asks, "Are they worthy?" as with adults.

If any calamity strikes a city, every strong heart, both bad and good, kind and unkind, cries, "Spare the children."

They are the caskets of the fondest hopes, the highest ambitions, the strongest love, the richest blessing, the most passionate prayer that ever earth records or heaven recognizes.

Who can estimate the wealth of worth caged in a little child? In the case of thousands the little soul starts out on the measureless tracks of an endless way with a whole army of forces behind it that can never die--the birth consecration, the cradle prayers, the mother's love.

But is there any line by which we can fathom the depths of the ocean of God's love for them? We read how by personal word He healed the outstretched withered hand; how by the touch of His sacred finger, He made the blind to see; how He permitted the penitent sinner to drop her tears upon His feet, and with her long black tresses to dry them; how He sat down and ate with the despised and hated tax-gatherer. But the children, He gathered into His arms, and nestled their heads upon His bosom, while He sealed all childhood sacred when His hands He laid on their heads.

And what should be more appealing to all that is best and strongest in us than the defenselessness of another? They have no voice to choose their lot; no power to resist the influences brought to bear upon them; no strength of heart or will to stand against the stream down which circumstances drift them.

They cannot find within their own resources the ability and decision which life demands. They cannot straighten out the crooked turns, or smooth the roughened places or light their own lamp to guide them amid the many pitfalls laid for their young feet.

Those which are not blessed at birth with a cradle with a prayer in it, or since birth with a home with a God in it, stand helpless amidst the tides of life's prevailing evils, and it is for us to press in between them and their adverse surroundings as heavenly guides.

We must not leave them alone to struggle with the early convictions of an awakening conscience. We must not leave them alone to define the rights and wrongs of the heart's many questions.

We must not leave them alone to hunt out how real and good and near God is. We must not leave them alone to wash from their little souls the heavy pollution cast on them by godless and wicked parents, for they cannot do it.

The fight is too hard, the night is too dark, the waters are too tempest-beaten. They can but go under, for they are helpless.

Do you know a child whom you consider to be a very wicked child? I say, throw a thousand excuses around his or her errings, for, if you hunt deep enough, you will find that a very whirlpool of currents has beaten against the little soul.

"Step in, Ma'am"

You could scarcely call it a house. A truer name would be hut, or shed. It was of earth color, and entirely void of any uniformity of structure. There was a door in the middle, fastened by a latch which lifted or fell, according to the adjustment of a dirty piece of string which hung on the inside.

There being no accounting for taste, one can never be sure what knowledge of good manners there may be hidden in the shabbiest abode, and so I thought I had better knock, and gave the wooden door a gentle tap.

The dirty piece of string evidently performed its accustomed duty, for the door flew open.

"Step in, ma'am," said the gentle voice of the small figure before me.

Such a fair little face, such a wan, wee form, such bony little hands; the only big things about this little seven-year-old girl were the large violet eyes peering through the uncombed ringlets framing the pinched features.

"Step in," she repeated, "step in, ma'am." And I did step in--right in, not only into the filthy, totally unfurnished room, but right into the dense darkness of the circumstances which cast their damning doom upon the helpless little soul before me.

Stretched upon a crude floor lay a woman, drunk.

"She is my mother," said the child, volunteering the information. "Father did not come home last night. A boy in the street said he was taken to the lock-up for striking a policeman. Mother is drunk just now. She is nearly always drunk. When I see her wake up I shall run away, 'cos I am very frightened of mother when she's drunk. Sometimes she knocks me down."

"Have you any brothers or sisters?" I asked. "No," was the quick reply. "I had one little sister once; she was a baby one; mother let her drop when she was drunk one day, and the doctor said it did something to her head that made her die. I was awfully sorry, cos I used to like to play with her and carry her about, and I am sure she liked me more better than mother, 'cos she held to my frock ever so when mother came."

The frock referred to was composed of two large patches, one an old piece of dark brown serge, the other a bit of gray flannel, bearing a strong yellow hue, testifying to having undergone a process of severe scorching. The two were sewn together with white cotton, and tied on with string.

All the way home through that long dreary journey the little gentle face, with the large, appealing eyes, was before me, and the words, "Step in"--asking us to step in between them and their godless conditions; in between them and the dark shadows of midnight circumstances; in between them and threatening destruction of all classes and characters.

Looking away from this incident for a moment, I look into the eyes of the hundreds within our own ranks, whom God has called to leap into the breach, and who have faltered and held back by the consideration of some selfish gain or the consciousness of some human weakness. Stretching out a hand of love and faith I catch your trembling one and would ask you, would persuade you, would entreat you to leap over every obstacle, and by the strength of omnipotence, and the grace of Calvary and the love of Christ Jesus, to turn your face towards this staring gap, and "Step in."

To the Army's Young People

A letter from the General

From The War Cry (New York), February 1935.

My dear young comrades:

Wide open doors of opportunity--ripened and ripening harvest fields--are everywhere, in every land, before our Army. My eyes are filled with the great and thrilling vision, and my mind and heart are burdened with thoughts of the vast moral and spiritual needs of the world today.

Teeming multitudes in our great cities, in towns and villages, are without Christ. They are trooping down to the immeasurable darkness without the true knowledge of God and His holy law, ignorant of His redeeming love for them.

Whole races and continents of men, women and little children are barely touched by the Gospel. The pity and the tragedy of it stirs my heart with passionate longing for a world-wide revival, a mighty, heaven-inspired forward movement to reach them. But we need officers!

The Master Calls

I will go still further and say that if your soul has heard the call of God to drop the tools of your daily work and to offer yourself for service at the battle's front, the Master needs <u>You</u>.

If your lips have been touched with the live coal, and your heart has been softened by Calvary's appeal, and your spirit has been illumined by the "light that never shone on land or sea," surely you will not hold back?

I cannot imagine how you dare hold back from a full consecration of all you are and all you hope for to help save a poor dying world!

Suppose Jesus had held back in the presence of Gethsemane's bitter cup and Golgotha's cruel cross! Think of the loss to the world, the loss for you, the loss for me, the loss for us all!

Suppose, for a moment, the apostles had clung to their nets and their tax-gathering, when called by the Master. How God's plans would have been defeated!

Suppose the veterans of the cross who blazed a trail for the Christian religion all over the world, gladly sacrificing their lives in so doing, had been so timorous of spirit and fearsome of mind as to hang back and disobey God's call! The world's evangelization would have been set back thousands of years.

But let me come nearer to your hearts.

Suppose my father, our beloved Founder, had refused to dedicate all there was of him to the poor, struggling and sin-bound masses. Where would have been the mighty, uplifting force, honored of God and man, with its globe-wide arms of mercy wrapped around the sorrowful and unchristianized of every clime, which is known as The Salvation Army? And without the Army, where would you yourself have been?

Has there ever a doubt entered your mind that God does not call men and women today as in the days that are past?

If so, I entreat you, put it away from you. It is the archenemy's subtle deception.

So long as there is spiritual need, so long as men and women and boys and girls are living and dying in sin, the call comes loud and clear and insistent.

Have you, yourself, heard it? If so, be honest with your own heart and conscience, and admit that you have.

When You Heard

You heard the call when the inebriated man ambled his way to your side and asked you to pray for him. You heard it when that poor girl wept bitter tears when you sang something about home and mother.

You heard the call at the funeral of that saintly officer, when his sword was laid down that he might receive the crown, making a vacant place in the Army's ranks.

You saw the need, perhaps as never before, at Christmastide with its mighty revelation of want and woe, and the Salvation Army's brave attempt to meet it.

You felt, "what a blessed work! I ought, I really ought, to give myself up entirely to it!" That was the call of God.

Let me persuade you not to halt, not to hesitate, not to let the glorious opportunities for time and eternity slip by.

The one thought in my mind at the moment is: "How much more could be done toward saving the world if more of our bright, capable, devoted young men and women, looking to Calvary for their passion for souls, would enlist in the ranks of officership?"

Self is the only prison door that can ever bind the soul;
Love is the only angel who can bid the gates unroll;
And, when He comes to call thee, arise and follow fast;
His way may lead through darkness, but it leads to light at last.

The Prophets and Apostles

Only obedience will preserve harmony between your will and God's will, and bring you into the sphere where your life will produce its best and holiest fruit.

If you feel your lack of fitness, of talent, of education, of knowledge and wisdom, remember that Moses felt just the same. So did Jeremiah. So did Paul. Your weakness will cast you upon God. He will not fail you. He will be with you as He was with Joshua, as He was with Isaiah, as He was with Paul.

Come along, come along to the battle today! Make your application at once to your commanding officer, or to the candidates' secretary at territorial headquarters.

Your General, depending upon you,

EVANGELINE BOOTH.

Chapter Three
The Challenge to Evangelism

War!

Declaration Of a New Offensive, Published by International Headquarters (London), circa 1935-1936.

Whereas certain information has been placed before me by the Commanders of the Forces of The Salvation Army operating in the ninety Countries and Colonies in which our Blood and Fire Flag has been unfurled, to the effect that the Prince of the Powers of the Air, the Father of Lies, the King of the Nethermost Regions, has failed utterly to fulfil the promises contained in the declaration he made to our first parents:

And the serpent said...Ye shall not surely die: For God doth know that in the day ye eat thereof, then your eyes shall be opened, and ye shall be as gods, knowing good and evil (Gen. 3:4,5).

And Whereas he has repeated again and again to the poor deluded slaves of sin whom he leads captive the promise that he would provide them with peace, prosperity, happiness, and security from all harm and death, and has as often disappointed them:

That old serpent, called the Devil, and Satan, which deceiveth the whole world (Rev. 12:9).

And Whereas in entering upon this vain and hopeless pursuit at his instigation these slaves of sin have been cruelly deceived, bound in fetters of transgression and remorselessly dragged from the paths of godliness, virtue, honesty, sobriety and truth:

He feedeth on ashes: a deceived heart hath turned him aside, that he cannot deliver his soul (Isaiah 44:20).

And Whereas, having broken the promises of the said declaration, and instead thereof having, under the guise of Worldly Fashion, Pride, Pleasure, and other intoxicating delusions, betrayed, decoyed, ensnared and destroyed thousands of precious souls for the Salvation of whom the Son of God shed His Blood upon Calvary:

Ye are of your father the devil, and the lusts of your father ye will do. He was a murderer from the beginning, and abode not in the truth, because there is no truth in him (John 8:44).

And Whereas the most brutal assaults are constantly being made upon innocent men, women and children by the slaves and agents of the Evil One, robbing them of character, virtue, hope, happiness and Heaven, and degrading them by compelling them by force, or deceiving them by lies, to become drunkards, harlots and vagabonds, thus bringing the sorrow, despair and misery of broken hearts, wrecked homes and early graves upon poor, defenseless, helpless little children and long-suffering wives and parents, besides hurrying his slaves and agents themselves to fill prison cells, people insane asylums, meet the murderer's doom and the suicide's fate, or to stagger down to the grave drunken, depraved, dishonored:

His own iniquities shall take the wicked himself, and he shall be holden with the cords of his sins (Proverbs 5:22).

And Whereas, further, information having been placed before me that these monstrous and sustained atrocities, appalling in their character, increase in number of violence, robbing the Church of God of its members, inducing soldiers to desert the Army of the Lord, destroying that which is best and most beautiful of an all-wise Creator's works of wonder and love, insulting the messengers of peace, crucifying the Son of God afresh, robbing Heaven of gems bought by Calvary's lamb to adorn the Royal Diadem:

The assemblies of violent men have sought after my soul; and have not set Thee before them (Psalm 86:14).

And Whereas, it having been represented to me that babes born in purity, and children with merry eyes and laughing lips, who rightly belong to God are in their childhood's innocence, being trained for the service of sin and Satan by godless, worldly parents who, themselves deceived by the arts and devices of King Beelzebub, unconscious of their own danger and that of their children, allow them to grow up to receive the wages of sorrow and

68

remorse and unless delivered from the hands of the enemy, to curse God and their parents and to die in their sins:

Whatsoever a man soweth, that shall he also reap (Galatians 6:7).

And Whereas, far exceeding in gravity any of the considerations already named inasmuch as it is at the root of every ill that mankind has brought upon itself, the Evil One has seduced the world from allegiance to its Creator, with the result that God is blasphemed, His Grace flouted, His Word ignored and efforts made to destroy His majesty:

Know therefore and see that it is an evil thing and bitter, that thou hast forsaken the Lord thy God, and that my fear is not in thee, saith the Lord God of Hosts (Jeremiah 2:19).

And Whereas everywhere can be found human hearts that vainly struggle against the whirlwinds of disappointment, loneliness, loss, broken things and troubled consciences.

Vanity of vanities; all is vanity (Ecclesiastes 1:2).

And Whereas beneath the billows of the infinite sea of sorrow, the natural and direct outcome of sin, a multitude of souls sink never to rise:

There they cry, but none giveth answer (Job 35:12).

69

And Whereas it has been represented to me that everywhere there is heart-hunger for God and soul-thirst for the truth that can never perish, I, Evangeline Booth, General of The Salvation Army, in the Name of God the Father, the rightful King and Ruler of the Universe; and in the Name of Jesus Christ, His Son, "Who taketh away the sin of the world," and whose servant and soldier I am; and by the gracious aid of the Holy Spirit, do hereby declare **a New Offensive**, in character more desperate and sustained than heretofore, against the combined forces of darkness commanded by the great Deceiver, King Beelzebub.

Thus saith the Lord unto you, Be not afraid nor dismayed by reason of this great multitude; for the battle is not yours, but God's (2 Chronicles 20:15).

This is to declare, therefore, that the Forces of The Salvation Army now enter upon a special, intensified Campaign for the Glory of God and the Salvation of Sinners. This, which will be continued until December 31, 1936, will be known as:
THE WORLD FOR GOD CAMPAIGN.
In this great effort I invite the prayers, sympathy and cooperation of all who love God and their fellows, all who hate sin and the abominations of evil, in order to help in the bringing about of a great world-wide revival of religion:

Who is on the Lord's side? Let him come unto me (Exodus 32:26).

70

Not least, I urge all who know Him and His Love to seek by every means to demonstrate to the world the power of the Lord God Almighty to save from sin.

He is able...to save them to the uttermost that come unto God by Him, seeing He ever liveth to make intercession for them (Heb. 7:25).

The supreme purpose of this Campaign is the destruction of every kind of evil resulting from sin, such as greed, immorality, gambling, blasphemy, malice, hatred, murders, thefts, hypocrisy, cant, jealousy, cowardice, fashion, pride, conceit, selfishness, lying and, in short, every enemy of God and man:

For this purpose the Son of God was manifested, that He might destroy the works of the Devil (1 John 3:8).

With this in view, I command every Officer, Soldier and Recruit of The Salvation Army throughout the world to step into the line of our world-wide fighting host. Forward! the World for God!

We will rejoice in Thy Salvation, and in the name of our God we will set up our banners (Psalm 20:5).

71

The World for God Campaign

To all Salvation Soldiers. An outline of what each is expected to do.

Found in the Library of the School for Officers' Training, Suffern, N.Y., dated November 2, 1935. No information on publication.

It is important to the progress of "The World for God" Campaign that the Soldiery of The Salvation Army should understand what their General is expecting of them in connection therewith. I DO THEREFORE HERE AND NOW DECLARE that I am depending upon each and all for wholehearted devotion to the Cause as well as for special and particular service as hereinafter mentioned.

First and Foremost let me impress upon the personnel of The Salvation Army that "The World for God" Campaign is essentially a Soldiers' Battle. We shall fall far short of reaching our goal if the fighting is left to the General, to the Territorial or the Divisional Commanders, or even to the Corps Commanding Officers. Every Soldier must be in it. The pledge of our Campaign Song,

I give my heart,
I will do my part,

must be carried into action without reservation all down the ranks.

The following outlines the duties and service for which I depend upon every Soldier:

1.   I EXPECT--unless prevented by ill-health or other circumstances which make absence unavoidable-- soldiers to take part in open-air meetings.

All my life I have been a great believer in street meetings. My earliest warfare will testify to this, as also will many who stood with me before the massed crowds in the streets of London and witnessed the never-to-be-forgotten scenes of men and women seeking salvation while kneeling at the wheels of an old truck, or by boxes or chairs loaned to us for the occasion.

The motorcades that I have since been privileged to conduct have deepened my conviction that God's way of reaching the masses is still by sending His messengers into the highways and the byways, and that the choicest tabernacles for the proclamation of His grace are the wide open spaces, or the thronged thoroughfares of the great cities with their ceaseless procession of disappointed, miserable and sinning souls.

These have not only been the field from which the Army has garnered countless numbers of its rank and file, but our open-air work has contributed in great measure to the ranks of our most valued and foremost officers.

Among the Greathearts of the past who were first attracted to the Army through its street meetings are such men as Commissioners Cadman, Booth-Hellberg, Rees, Holz and Gifford, whose names are known around the world. The much- beloved Colonel James Barker, on the top of a bus, passed a Bethnal Green open-air meeting, was moved to get off and see what was taking place, followed the small group to the old Railway Arch and was saved that night.

The sight of an English-born Officer, clad in native garb, preaching Christ in the streets of Kandy, called the saintly Weerasooriya to comradeship with Commissioner Booth-Tucker in pioneering work in Indian villages and the saving of thousands of souls.

Men of wealth, struck by the devotion of a handful of Salvation Soldiers, and the earnestness of a message from a redeemed drunkard, or a saved domestic, have again and again been moved to make immediate gifts of money, and some to remember The Salvation Army in their wills, with the result that the divine service of the little group has been multiplied a hundredfold.

Millions of people, high and low, rich and poor, educated and illiterate, never hear a gospel hymn, or any other proclamation of salvation truth unless it is at our street meetings. A Salvation Army open-air gathering is the only touch of religion that enters their lives.

2.   I EXPECT the salvation soldier to attend indoor meetings; to hold himself ready to speak, to sing, or to pray; to render the valuable service of "fishing" in the prayer meetings; or to perform any other duty his commanding officer may assign to him.

3.   I EXPECT all who hold local officers' commissions to discharge in letter and spirit the duties they have

undertaken to perform, thereby demonstrating a worthy example of holy enthusiasm, and placing themselves in the lead in the great enterprises embraced in this campaign.

4.   I EXPECT bandsmen and songsters not only to seek to excel in their playing and singing, so that their performances may attract the people, but to make their songs and music of that character that shall awaken men and women to the dangers that beset the unconverted soul. Sanctified musical talent is one of the most powerful means God has given man to help in bringing the world to His feet.

5.   I EXPECT every soldier to do his full part to bless and save the young people. Remember that in blessing and helping a child, we bless and help not only what is, but what we hope for. With all my heart I urge that all who are able to do so will offer themselves to their corps commanding officer for duty in the young people's branch of our work.

6.   I EXPECT our soldiers to make use of every possible means of approaching people personally about their souls. In this connection, I make a special appeal to the Home League, to the Goodwill League, to all those who undertake the blessed ministry of hospital, prison, or slum visitation, for such will find special openings in "The World for God" Campaign for this greatest of all service.

7.   I EXPECT each soldier to hold himself responsible for persuading some one or more persons to attend the meetings, giving special attention to relatives of those already associated with the corps, such as members of the Young People's Companies, Life-Saving Scouts and Guards, Home League members, and others.

8.   I EXPECT all to wear the campaign button. I regard this as very important. It will advertise the fact that we are making a worldwide, concerted attack on the forces of evil and create a universal interest in the campaign. The button, also, signifies the unity of our effort upon every battlefield. A button on the coat of the last little African Recruit in South Africa links him in service with the foremost commissioners in our ranks--or with the General herself.

9.   I EXPECT all soldiers, and particularly those holding office as ward sergeants, to cooperate diligently with their officers in shepherding the flock. This is of vital importance, for I do not think you can find one instance in the Bible where a man was converted without God's calling in some human instrument or agent. Soldiers who may be neighbors, or work mates, of converts can render blessed and eternal service in this way--a service which, although possibly unseen and unknown by man, will be written in God's Book of Remembrance.

10.   I EXPECT every soldier to read *The War Cry*. They should read it (1) For the instruction it contains with regard to this campaign. (2) For the information it gives as to what God is enabling The Salvation Army to accomplish in every part of the world. (3) Because above everything else it is a messenger of salvation. (4) Because it is the General's only means of communicating with her people. (5) Because its every page carries educational instruction, spiritual edification, and that inspiration which is borne on the wings of song, of poetry and of music.

11.   Finally, I EXPECT every soldier to consecrate himself to God for the purposes of this world-wide Campaign. Those whom God accepts for His service He will consecrate with His Spirit for that service. Those whom He adopts into His family, He will anoint with the oil of His love. Those whom He makes sons He will make saints. For God does not only give His children a new name, but a new nature.

        If I can persuade our great Army of soldiery to throw themselves at the feet of the Savior with that abandonment with which Paul threw himself, crying, "What wilt Thou have me to do?" we shall achieve a victory in His Name that will shake the world. For God turns feebleness into might, slothfulness into dominating action and selfishness into reckless devotion to the good of others.

        "The King's business requireth haste."

Chapter Four
Reflections on Many Subjects

Colored Views

Charity...thinketh no evil; rejoiceth not in iniquity, but rejoiceth in the truth (1 Corinthians 13:5,6).

From The War Cry (Toronto), December 12, 1898. Reprinted in Love Is All, published by Reliance Trading Company (New York), 1908.

"Beauty is in the eye of the beholder." This there is no mistaking. Here is the reason for a mother thinking her babe the perfection of childhood's charms, and for a father seeing his son to be in possession of attractions of which few others can boast. Then, if beauty is so completely in the adoring eye, I should certainly say that the uncomely appearance presented by some people and things is also solely to do with the unfavorable vision of the beholder.

It is not a necessary sequence that there is nothing of an admirable nature in the object because it is not discerned by the onlooker. No matter with what magnificence and artistic correctness the scene may be portrayed on canvas, if the eye lacks the perception of harmonious blending of color, or the realistic grouping of life, to such a one the picture is but a poor, bedaubed affair, whereas to an eye quickened with a perception for the beautiful, it stands as a triumph of art.

Where there is a nonperception of harmony in sound, the impression left upon the ear by the most cultured music will be that of discord. The other day I heard of a gentleman whose friends took him to a string concert of exceptional renown. After listening to the rare rendering of classical strains on the violin and cello for quite a little while, he remarked, "When are they going to begin? What a time they have been tuning up their instruments!"

And so I say that the world of music, art and creature is largely what our perceptiveness makes it. For it is a hard matter to discern or appreciate that which finds nothing akin to our own souls, or in other words, an easy matter to cast the reflection of a sunny and glorious nature, or the shadow of an evil and suspicious mind, over the deeds and lives of others.

Now, in this "Thinketh no evil," I am reminded of a qualification of charity, which beautifies everything, and at the same time of an appalling weakness which has destroyed the happy experience of many.

This spirit of evil possessing the mind is no respecter of persons. We find it in all classes, and squeezing its way in despite all manner of professions. There are thinkers of evil in every church, in every society, in every Salvation Army hall, although it is one of the most destructive and poisonous besetments to which the soul and a religious society can be subjected. It tends to make cliques and form sects in all communities, disbanding the unity of the whole. It saps the spiritual influence of the individual soul. It undermines and confounds the strongest and purest trust.

I have known one evil-thinker to overthrow a whole church--to thrust back the Christian of long years' standing--to entrap the innocent and simple, and to drag the Blood and Fire Flag through a gutter of ignominy, into which no rampant persecution could have lowered it. I have no hesitancy in saying that evil thinking is a damnable sin.

How are such people distinguished? Easily! Not because of their being so numerous, but because their faultfinding spirit is so clearly manifested in such multitudinous forms and shapes. Their attitude is suspicious, and their expression bespeaks an officious desire to peer into the secret chambers held in every heart. Their conversation is fluent and excited--they are never hard up for a story to tell; they show no delicacy in parading the misfortunes of others; they are scarcely ever stuck fast for the beginning or the ending of a tale; they can always add either, and exaggerate the middle.

They think that they polish their own virtues by enlarging upon the faults of others. They seldom take people to mean what they seem, unless that seeming goes unfortunately against them; for they impute base motives for even virtues. They rejoice in iniquity and not in the truth.

When a sorely-tempted soul goes down and under, they say, "I told you so," and with great liberty propound the advisability of running on the French maxim, "Doubt all men till you prove them true." They can find the flaw in every gem, the cloud in every sky, the fault in every life, and see many that were never there, and never will be.

I see that evil-thinking makes us hard and unjust to those who labor in our interests, or under our authority. Somebody I was speaking to the other day said that they had never met anyone who came up to their ideal of religion--that there was "none good, no, not one;" the Christians were no better than others, but rather worse, being the bearers of an empty profession. And the speaker instanced in support of these melancholy conclusions one or two of whom she once thought well, but who afterwards showed themselves (as she termed it) in their true character.

There was a minister whom she deemed wickedly proud of his good preaching, although so fervent and earnest were his sermons that he would often faint at the conclusion of his heaviest services; and there were many others with whom she found serious fault.

But a salvation servant was the last to fall under her scathing suppositions, for she said, "When Mary does hurry on with the work and gets through things quickly and neatly, it is only to be off to the meetings, or out seeking her own in some other respect;" although she admitted that Mary was the most trustworthy girl she had in the house.

I thought, as she alighted from the car, *What a perverted mind--what an absence of charity--what a spectacle of ugliness of character to which evil-thinking can reduce one!*

Again, I see that evil-thinking makes us hard and unjust to those who are above us. I know those whom circumstances are all that can be desired. God has not only seemed to bless them, but favored them. He has given them companionship, home, comforts and influences. Their wages are good and reasonable.

But they complain. They nurse the feeling that they are hardly done by. They suspect the expressed inability of their employers to do better. They say he could if he would. They accuse him of a grudge toward themselves, and partiality to others. They feel badly toward those over them. They embitter their own lives whether or not they affect anyone else's when they have all reason to feel well. They are thinkers of evil. They are ensnared by that abominable sin which lies at the root of three parts of the ingratitude which, in its blindness to advantages, often throws overboard the brightest of future prospects.

Then, evil-thinking makes us hard and unjust on those who are on equal standing with us--our comrade in the strife, our friend on the path of life, our neighbor who, remembering the commands of God, has every claim upon our merciful consideration. But the ten thousand blessings that should be bestowed upon those climbing with us the steeps of time are interfered with by these evil suspicions and dark surmisings.

The man who is occupied by revolving in his mind, let alone turning over with his tongue, the weakness which he fancies can be detected in the faltering steps or the impeded journey of another, will be the last to extend a helping hand to assist a weaker than himself. Or the woman, be she a Salvationist or a constant pewholder, who has ever ready a whisper detrimental to the family whose name is up at the moment, will be the last to staunch the wound of a bleeding heart or bind a breaking spirit.

I write with much sorrow that in my experience I have known many whose one and only besetting sin could be classified as *evil-thinking*. It may have been a bestower of goods to feed the poor, or a Salvationist, a member of the church, a frequent open-air attender, or a good public speaker--yet all the same an *evil-thinker*. They hold on to a bit of discreditable back history of every convert which they think should be remembered; they can always throw in words calculated to hang weights on those lifted in praise of anyone. They say, "It is not what people seem, it is what they are," and leave others to wonder what they mean, while they work hard behind the scenes to undo any good impression made in the party's favor.

When they cannot circulate actual evil reports, they cast cruel insinuations, such as, "Beware of so-and-so," or with a significant nod of the head, infer that there are "dark things which they would speak, but charity makes them forbear," when in reality there are no dark things but in their own dark minds. Thus they build almost insurmountable barriers for many young and trembling feet which have already more than enough in the cold currents of life to struggle against.

Evil-thinkers hold not back from tearing holes in the garments of the most needy and helpless. I had scarcely said, "Oh, what a dear, motherly and sympathetic soul that woman is!" when someone overhearing my remark whispered: "Oh, she has a dreadful temper; is so fearfully irritable that I sometimes even wonder if the old soul knows what conversion means." Personal observations, however, made me detect that the woman criticized prayed much more fervently in the meetings for the souls of others than my staring-about informant, and on inquiry I learned that the former was a widow, with six children, who buried her husband seven years ago, when her youngest was an infant of two or three months.

All through the long seven years with bony fingers, rounded shoulders, burdened head and breaking heart, this mother in her widowhood had earned the bread and clothes for the six orphans. I could not help thinking when I heard the story, that even were it so that, owing to overtaxed

84

nerves and overwearied limbs, this woman was guilty of sharp-speaking, how much more excusable to the Friend of the widow in whom the "fatherless findeth mercy" was her irritable tongue than the ceaseless fault-finding of the backbiting one. Instead of this evil-thinking being a slight offence, I see it to be a monstrous iniquity, hurting and blighting wherever its heavy and cruel feet tread.

The last remark I will make respecting evil-thinkers is that they must be more or less a very miserable class of people; I cannot see how it could be otherwise. They are dissatisfied with their surroundings, and their surroundings are dissatisfied with them; they see the evil in everybody, and, with isolated exceptions, everybody can see what a great deal of evil lodges in them. They point their fingers at the imaginary mote in every eye, and all around are painfully conscious of the crowd blocking up their own.

They have no real friends; none can sufficiently trust to befriend them; the general feeling is that no reputation, no matter how pure and blameless, is safe in their hands. They do not really love anyone, and while persisting in focusing their vision on the one small distant speck in every man's character, I do not see how we could expect to find many hearts that would risk love on them; did they, it would be as in the case of the servant girl, that base and selfish motives would be imputed, besmearing even virtue with the coloring of sin.

"When thine eye is single thy whole body is full of light." All this evil-thinking with the hard-heartedness, narrow-mindedness, disloyalty and self-deceivedness that it brings results from an unclean heart, making darkness within, and casting its black pall on all without. It is a sorrowful sin, it is a terrible fault, it is a cruel besetment, a spoiling of the past, a withering of the present, a blasting of the future course! If it is yours, run to Calvary, look to Jesus, see His face!

He thought the best possible of His murderers; He threw between their black guilt and the Father the only imaginable excuse in the cry, "they know not what they do." Seek His love, learn of His pity, ask His compassion, plead His grace, and while in the revealing light of a blameless Christ, bearing the guilt and shame of a world's sin, pour hot condemnation on your every unkind thought, harsh judgment, evil suspicion and unmerciful conclusion, and seek charity--which power alone can deliver you from the ruin in time and curse in eternity--of this hell-forged snare of the human mind--evil-thinking.

Then - Face to Face

*Weeping may endure for a night, but joy cometh in the
morning (Psalm 30:5).*

From The War Cry (New York), January 1, 1916.

There is to be an inestimable and indescribable
difference between our present day and our eternal
tomorrow. Today the heavy shadows falling from sin,
mystery and grief; tomorrow the golden breaking of
cloudless light from the once-marred visage. We are to
enter into His presence; we are to stand before His throne;
we are to look upon His countenance; nothing between, no
glass, no cloud, no time intervening, but "face to face" with
Jesus, Jesus who came, Jesus who lived, Jesus who
suffered, Jesus who died. Now the hazed and beclouded
view, then a fadeless shining!

Now the tumult and the strife,
Then the rest--eternal life!
Now the weeping and the sighs,
Then the song and the tearless eyes!

Now the children dying, then no more parting! Now
the waters dividing, then no more sea! Now the grave's
hearts breaking, then the resurrection greeting! Now the
night winds chilling and killing, then the morning lifting
and brightening! Morning on the mountains! Morning on

the plains! Morning with an eternity in it! Morning--
Morning!

Oh, the transforming touch of that hour! Only
intelligence irradiated by contact with the skies could give
us to recognize our heaviest cross, when it comes to crown
us there. We shall find our failures; they will greet us as
triumphs. We shall find our bereavements; they will meet
us as reunions. We shall find our loss rebounding in
eternal gain. We shall find our hidden struggles crowned
in open victory. We shall find our hottest tears forming
coronation gems. We shall find the complete fulfillment of
every promise of the Bible, the realizing of the highest
hopes of the righteous, the verifying of the fondest dreams
of the saints. Face to face with Jesus; the gates of strife
closed behind us, the boundary crossed; the veil torn; the
morning broken.

The light gets brighter and brighter, as on the wing of
revelation I climb the heights before me, and, looking
through the dazzling brilliancy which only the eye of
immortality can gaze into, see the massive multitude of
which John says all attempts at calculation fail to estimate.
All eyes are lifted to the starry lettering writing the
meanings of life's every mystery.

Now these orphans see why mother and father both are
taken, leaving them to tears and the cold world all alone.
Now they even smile and sing, and say it was best. How
glad that mother is now that the children went on first!
Their little feet would have been too badly torn in life's
thorny ways. That wife sees the reasons for the struggles
of a long widowhood as clear as the shining of the Golden
Gate. The saints of the hospital thank God for all the

suffering. The bearers of the cross thank Him for the persecution; Paul, for the scourged back; Silas, for the prison cell; Ridley, for the flames, and Catherine of Sienna, for prison flags.

They all say it was best; it was best, it was the dawning of the most triumphant glory in disguise. Suffering is the only ladder long enough to lift us from our low levels on earth to thrones in Heaven.

Then I hear a great sound, like as the roar of many waters; as out of the numberless multitudes of all nations, kindreds, peoples and tongues. Then a thousand mothers lift their voices and shout: "Blessings to our God which sitteth upon the throne! He spread His wings over my nursery and blessed my children." Others shout, "Wisdom! He enlightened my ignorance, and by His truth taught me." Others, "Thanksgiving! He blotted out as a thick cloud my transgressions and covered my sin." Others, "Honor! He gathered me from the disgrace of the outcast and redeemed my name." Others, "Power! He gave me the victory over every foe." Others, "Might! He touched my weakness and turned it into greatness."

Then the harps are strung and the seraphims sing, and the angels strike the key-note, while all the children clap their hands. Sight unequaled, sound unparalleled, light unrivaled, as the heavenly orchestra catches the strain of the numberless multitude and burst in with the chorus of the Hallelujah Anthem, singing, "Blessing, and glory, and wisdom, and thanksgiving, and honor, and power, and might, be unto our God forever and ever! Amen."

Oh, it is the "face-to-face" time! No one can describe the glory. It is the crowning. It is Jesus--Bosrah's Hero,

Calvary's Lamb, Resurrected Lord, the sinner's Savior. Again the redeemed break out as every eye is cast on the wounded hands, the riven side, the thorn-pierced brow of the conquering Lord!

Worthy is the Lamb, who on Calvary was slain. All along the line of march, they are waving the palms, for the Bride stands forth--the Church of God adorned in redemption's glory, while all heads that were weary in the conflicts of righteousness are crowned; hearts that were true to their calling, crowned; lives that reflected His likeness, crowned; souls washed white in His Blood, crowned. All nations at the banquet--from all places of the earth. They have pressed through the waters; they have stood in the fires; they have fought with the beasts; they have lived and died in dungeons.

There is Stephen who was stoned. There is James who was clubbed. There is Matthew who was flogged. There is Paul who was whipped and imprisoned and beheaded, and multitudes more who suffered for Jesus. They stand in the light; their garments are white; their faces are bright; they sing, they shout, they shine; they are Home; they are at the banquet; they are with Jesus; they are "face to face." No more pain, no more death, no more hunger, no tear, no sigh, no grave, no night; all morning!--The Bridal Morning--"The Bridal Morning of The Lamb!"

This Lovely World

From The War Cry (Chicago), July 31, 1937.

This is a beautiful world--indescribably beautiful. Before its architectural grandeur and its artistic design, revealing the incomparable genius of its Creator, the best accomplishments of man pale into insignificance. Its mountains of rock, lifting above castles of cloud their suncrowned heads, level to the dust the most magnificent productions of the sculptor's chisel. Its blend of harmonious coloring in bird's wing, in sky blue, in snow crystal and beach coral, bewilder the wildest fancies of the painter's brush. Its captivating music, throbbing through the heart of the hills, is beyond comparison with that of the master musicians of all ages.

Great orchestras, by the skillful manipulation of instruments and exquisite interpretation of the composer's sentiments, hold vast audiences spellbound and sway their emotions. But what artists can be compared with those whom God files into the galleries of the forest to play a wedding march as all Nature breaks forth into song?

Joy of trees, hurrying on their garments of shimmering green; joy of fishes flashing their silver and gold and purple through the waters; joy of insects--artisan, architect, and artist insects--racing through a thousand activities in the sand. Joy of wings in the sky; joy of beasts in newly-adorned forest; joy of cattle on a thousand hills; joy of cataract and waterfall and rivulet, laughing themselves dizzy as they clash their crystal heels on pebbled paths. All this music is the thrill of God's heart; all the color of blue and green and purple and saffron and rose is but the reflection of His beauty.

I read omnipotence in every blade of grass; the wooing of His love in every robin's call; divine purity in every lily; God's almighty, cleansing power in every wave of the sea; a triumphal arch in every tree branch. I see Eternal Majesty, God, Omnipotence, Creator, mighty and magnificent, riding in chariot of stars across every sky; and yet I see all heaven contained in a dewdrop.

Do we not want to put our trust in this same great God? Will not He who cares for the young in the sparrow's nest look after our children also, if we trust Him? Will not this same great God who "hath made the earth by His power," guard our best interests if we commit them to His care?

If you are a sinner, He will be your Savior. If you have wandered, He will bring you home. A friend of mine told me that his gardener one day, while attending to his duties, noticed a small bird circling round and round, uttering shrill cries of distress. He quickly saw that it was pursued by a hawk, but before he could render any assistance the little wounded creature, exhausted by exertion and terror, fell at his feet. The gardener lifted it and found that it was torn and bleeding. He placed it in his breast, sheltering it with the warm folds of his coat, and nursed it back to health. The little thing, when offered its freedom, would not leave the gardener, but always preferred for its resting place, his coat.

I tell you that our Lord Jesus is not an austere monarch who can only be approached by elaborate ceremony and strictest adherence to court etiquette. He is One who stands in our pathway that He may shield us from the trouble and the enemies that pursue us, and hide us and shelter us beneath the folds of His mantle.

This glorious summertime, when every rose is a very carnival of color, every leaf a creature of beauty, every flower a perfection, every bird a praise, every tree a psalm, every upturned petal a prayer, I beg of you to tune your heart to the music of God's Universe and to let His love, revealed to us in our Savior Jesus Christ, flood your soul with new life and glory.

Chapter Five
Alcoholism--Prohibition

Drink's Triple Trail

Drink's World, Drink's Work, Drink's Woe

From The War Cry (Toronto), February 25, 1899.

Drink's World

Its paths, inlaid with snare and ruin, run from the highest and most cultured places of our most enlightened lands, down through the darkest alleys of poverty and pauperism and into the lowest vaults of infamy and vice. There is no thoroughfare so wide, no hut so desolate, no cave so hidden, no nation so fair, no strand so laden with disastrous wreck, but where the heavy tread of this monster, Drink, with either the wail of destruction in its tramp, or with its venomous sting hidden by its deluding glare, has been heard in its funeral march.

It dwells in marble halls. The most gorgeous tapestry bedecks its chambers. The walls through which it glides are spacious and imposing. It is no stranger to the art of the most beautiful, the most elaborate skill. The floors over which its stealthy feet glide are often marble, the ceilings of gilded fretwork, the frescoed walls upon which it casts its shadows are of mahogany and satinwood. Its blazing gas-jets in globes of dainty hues hang from massive brackets. Its ear is accustomed to the sweetest strains of most cultured music, into which it will only too surely introduce all the dirges of minor keys. Its envious eye rests with ravishing greed upon the beauteous form of fairest

95

creature, and the most elegant spread of glorious nature and most artistic skill displayed in picture, with thirst to cast its blight on all.

Infanticide and Suicide

A lady, extravagantly dressed, holding by the hand a sweet little boy of some six years, also displaying all taste and plenty in his attire, accompanied by a nurse with a fair baby of six months in her arms, attended one of my more select meetings in the Old Country. She seemed to take something of a fancy to me, and waited to speak to me at the conclusion of the meeting. I felt some affinity with her--perhaps it was the hidden sorrow, of which I knew nothing, drew in an imperceptible way upon my sympathy. But we talked happily over a cup of tea, in the vestry; I kissed the children, prayed with them and blessed them.

We met occasionally after this. I was to have gone to her home, but never found the time. She frequently sent the little boy to see me, and the only thing that impressed me strangely was when asking of his father, the nurse became very agitated, and would change the conversation. One night, at the conclusion of a large meeting, to my surprise, I found the nurse sitting in the lobby, with a face white as death. I asked why she did not come into the meeting, and enquired the reason of her being out with the boy at such a late hour; she burst into bitter wailing; I could get no response to my questions. Turning to the boy, I asked if his mother was sick. He replied:

"No! Nurse cries because mother has gone away with baby."

Then the girl, burying her head in her hands, said: "Oh! My mistress has gone to jail."

"To jail?" I gasped.

"Yes! she has killed the baby; she put laudanum in its milk by mistake. She was drunk."

A letter afterwards told me she had committed suicide.

Yes! they fall as a star from the very heavens--to a cinder in hell.

But drink stays not there. It sits at the hearth of the humbler home; it gazes with hideous smile upon the honest toil for bread; it creeps upstairs; it glitters on the table in the little festivities of the happy home, lurking behind the damnable argument of the harmlessness of moderate drinking, while with hungering designs it lays its plans with careful calculation as to the little time it will take to snatch the pretty blue frock from the little form, and the pretty pink flush from the little cheek, the good warm boots from the little feet, the carpet from the floor, and the clock from the shelf; the gladness from the mother's eye, and the honor from the father's heart; the bread from the cupboard, and the fire from the grate.

But drink stays not there! Through the courts and alleys its blood-besmeared feet hasten with a rapidity only lent to absolute and complete destruction; down into the cellars, up into the garrets; hid away in sheds; in any and every hole that can shelter want and woe are to be found crawling, standing, sitting, leaning, kneeling, treading, the slaves and victims of this dark passion--*Drink!* Their faces are drawn with agony; their reasons distorted with crime; their names are blighted with shame; their homes are gone; their characters are gone--all over the counter for beer, all into the hotel-keeper's till, all into the brewer's pocket.

But Drink stays not here. It is the shadow behind the garish footlights of the stage. It is the demon glare thrown into the brilliancy of the ballroom. It is the frenzied fascination of the gambling-table. Its playthings are the fair babes of our cradles; its merriment the tears of our wronged and bereaved; its sport the haunted consciences of wretched man, and the delirious wanderings of maddened minds; its nature the blood of its victims.

Its sky is blackened with the pall of death; its rivers a multitude of fallen tears; its atmosphere thickened with the wail of suffering. *Drink is a Dragon* thirsting for human blood! *It is a Monster* with a rabid lust for human life! *It is a Pestilence* which paralyzes the will, bewilders the brain! *It is a Flame,* scorching and withering all it touches! It is the most active, the most powerful, the most successful enemy of the soul, for it is not one sin, it is *all!* Crushing the old, cursing the young, and blighting even the children.

The Demon of Drink says with Napoleon: "Give me the children, and I will conquer the world."

Drink's Work

It *is gradual*. Almost all drunkards were once moderate drinkers. There has never been known a man who has intended to be mastered by this power. The supposed harmlessness of the one glass has been the damnation of body and soul for a thousand times ten thousand men. Oh, this tasting of father's glass with the children, this having it in the cupboard, this countenancing and patronizing in part of what on the whole is a worldwide traffic of destruction, has just been the lighting of the fires which have consumed three parts of earth's best and brightest.

Of all arguments which to my mind are the most base in their gross distortions of natural reason, their contradiction of all conscience-dictates, an annihilation of all manly honor, are those which would plead in favor of drink in moderation, as though the fact of taking the death-drug in small quantities could change its nature-- which nature is restless, untiring pursuit until all is devoured and destroyed.

Is hell heaven, because hell
In little drops be given?

Oh, the thousands of young men who start with no greater desire or intention than to be in the fashion. They take the first glass in the high-class hotels of the city, but they have linked hands with the monster; the grasp becomes tighter and tighter, until the touch of the friend is lost in the grip of the fiend. Listen! The clock strikes twelve! It is the death-knell of a soul; the gas-jets intermingle their lights with the bleared glare of the youth; the flush of his cheek is the breath of eternal woe. The saloon-keeper cuffs him, waking him from his drunken slumber, says it is time to close, throws him out. He's down. He's damned! He began a moderate drinker in a first-class hotel. He finishes his dissipation an inveterate drunkard in the lowest saloon.

99

Banish the drink both in small and great quantities! Banish it from your homes, from your children, from your wives, from your tables, from your cities, and, God helping you, from this our fair country.

Five Years' Work

One of my officers was driving through one of the border streets in a city of this country.

Attention was drawn to a tall, slight figure on the sidewalk; a woman, who wore widows' weeds; her attire gave evidence of a continual effort to retain neatness. The skirt was brushed threadbare, the boots were patched, the little bonnet was extremely worn. The figure halted, gave a quick look round, then stooped and snatched from the gutter a crust--then another look round, and holding up her shawl to prevent all possible detection, began to gnaw away at the frozen bread.

The officer drew up the rig and sprang to her side saying, "You are hungry and in want. Can I help you?"

Her story was soon told. What a happy home, what a loving husband, what a beautiful baby she had once! "My lover, my sweetheart, my husband, my protector, my supporter, and my baby all carried away by the drink, sir-- in five short years."

My honored and sainted mother, in her writings, speaks about the drink traffic as follows:

But not only is abstinence valuable, nay, indispensable, in order to preserve those rescued out of the power of this great destroyer, but it is equally valuable to prevent others from falling into it.

We all profess to believe that prevention is better than cure. Seeing, then, that strong drink is proved to be the most dangerous foe to perseverance in righteousness, and the most potent cause of declension, inconsistency and apostasy, ought not Christians to strive, both by example and precept, to warn the young, the weak and the inexperienced from touching it?

Can any man answer for the consequences of putting a bottle to his neighbor's mouth--be it ever such a small one, or ever such a genteel one? God has recorded His curse against the man who does this, and thousands of hoary-haired parents, broken-hearted wives and weeping, blighted children groan their "Amen" to the dreadful sentence.

Perchance there are some men who can take these drinks in what they call moderation, and suffer no visible injury; nevertheless, let that man beware who touches that which God cursed, for there are injuries invisible more to be dreaded than all the plagues of Egypt!

It is complete! I was just about ready to leave a city lately visited by me, when a lady stepping from a carriage was ushered into my room. Her countenance was of exceptional beauty, her apparel was of costly worth, her speech denoted education and refinement. Putting out her hand she said, "My apology for taking up your time, Miss Booth. It was my anxiety to speak to the only woman that has ever made me cry, and this I did all through your address last night." A few minutes talk revealed the reason of the hot tears referred to.

101

The story ran much on all those things which used to be: loving home, beautiful nursery, the mother's care, the gentle training, the happy marriage and then, always having been a moderate drinker, drink in greater quantities was the only receipt for relief from the grief and unexpected sorrow. And with bated breath and staring eye, she whispered, "It is the drink, Miss Booth! It has driven my husband from me, locked up my children in the convent, spent my fortune; it has shut the doors of my home, blasted my character, robbed my virtue--and now I am down past the reach of any man, and even God Himself." And she gathered her cloak around her, and before I could speak she said, "I must go; you may tell my story to as many as you like. It may save some other creature who is as fair as I once was fair, from becoming as black as I now am black."

I say the work of drink is complete. It not only throws overboard every enjoyable feature of circumstances, running with the library and instruments to the pawnbrokers. But what is much more to be prized, he strips the subject himself of his priceless treasure, puts his hand down on reason and turns it into imbecility. He puts his hand down on honor--honor with which none can part without bitter agony, and turns it to shame; puts its hand down on truth and turns it to craft and falsehood; puts its hand down on beauty and so mars, scars, tears and hacks until no trace of loveliness can be found.

It stays not at taking the bloom from the cheek, but goes on until the death breezes fan it; it stays not at bent back, round shoulders, curved spine, and fractured limbs, but goes on until it lays the body in the grave. Complete in its ruin of body, soul and mind!

I knew of a garret absolutely empty, but for the suffering form of a drunken woman and a few rags.

The birth of the baby boy that morning brought with it no maternal affection, but only the fervent prayer that it would die; not a rag was prepared for the unwelcome mite; its first bath was in the boiler, and its first covering part of an old garment torn from the back of his little sister. However, the poor little babe persisted in living, in spite of these unwelcome circumstances, and nine days afterwards appeared with its mother in the county court. The fact of the matter was that all the furniture had gone to meet the infuriated demands of the unpaid landlord, but did not nearly satisfy the amount due.

"How can you pay this account?" asked the judge of the woman. Diving her hands underneath the tattered shawl which covered her otherwise bare shoulders, she drew forth her naked babe, and holding it forth at her bony arm's length said, "You can take this if you like!"

The woman afterwards was heard to sob out in the ears of her dark world's one friend, "I wor so mad that I hardly knew what I wor doin'."

Drink's Woe

Who can tell its story? What pen could write its tale? What heart could cry the griefs of drink and woe?

Look at this procession if we can. Let God touch our imagination and help us to do so.

Their tread is ever languid, their faces never smile; their hearts are ever bleeding. Each day for them but brings new curses: new brutality, new hunger, new fear, and new dread.

If they pray, then with every awakening morning and every setting sun they ask God, the Creator, by pity of the sorrow, to number them with the dead.

A crowded court in Toronto--this city--in the prisoner's box stands a forlorn and desperate looking woman, a creature to whom one blushes to give the name of woman.

No small consternation is caused by a police official carrying over a chair to place on the steps where the witnesses stand.

The tiny hand clinging to the strong fingers of a stalwart constable is that of a baby witness, only four years old, whose little frail form is lifted up on the chair. You might have thought the sunlight concentrated all its golden glory in the ringlets of the hair, the skin was of snowy complexion, the features pinched with want, but correctly marked, and the eyes two large windows for the soul to look through.

Little Maggie was her name; she was the child of the woman in the prisoner's dock. She had been swung round and round by the hair, in her mother's drunken rage, and was brought to show the wounds, a proof of the story.

"Did your mother do this?" the child was asked. The lips parted to answer in the affirmative, when the little face was lifted to the pitiable object opposite her. Seeing the woman standing between two big policemen, she took in her mother's woeful position, and lifting her large eyes to the judge with a trembling quiver in the baby lips, and the wound plainly showing in her head, she said, "No sir; my mother never did it, my mother never did it!"

What a revision of God's living purpose! A four-year old baby shielding and pleading for its mother!

This is not in a heathen land; this is in our own. This is in no barbarous country, this is on our doorstep; it runs through our streets. They are our own fair girls and our brave sons who sink beneath this dark tide, and are drawn into the vortex of this whirlpool!

Do I believe it? Yes, not only because I've heard so much of it, but because I've seen so much of it.

Why, only just near my own office, a little time back in this beautiful city, a father killed his own son by driving the mother's scissors into his heart. He was drunk. When sober, and told what he had done, he lost his reason with grief. Does it not behoove us, as Christian men and women, should it not compel our churches where the word of God is upheld, where righteousness is contended for, and solace of all grief proclaimed, should it not constrain us as a Christian country to arise, and equipping ourselves with the weapons of truth and righteousness with irresistible perseverance, strike out at the enemy in season and out of season, with a force which springs from the knowledge of this sin, and from the accumulated wrongs, oppressions, griefs, sorrows, tears of Drink's woe?

Strike out at Drink, this giant foe of virtue and peace with a hand that will not stay, and a heart that will not relent, and feet that will not halt until we have driven the enemy without our gates, and our land stands an example of soberness and happiness in the front rank of all the countries of the world.

Shall America Go Back?

Excerpted from a thirty-page pamphlet containing an address read before the National Convention of the Women's Christian Temperance Union at Philadelphia, 1922

Published by National headquarters (New York), (n.d.).

The Temperance Revolution

We are here today to mingle our voices in the shout of victory over what will ever be the world's greatest moral triumph. But we are still upon the field, not with our swords in their scabbards, but drawn to drive the remainder of the enemy beyond our gates, and to keep them there.

The enemy's line has, indeed, crumbled, and his citadel has been captured, but the discredited outlaw still essays a guerilla warfare, and I am quite sure that your Convention has resulted in renewal of purpose to attack, and then attack again, until the outlaw, drink, with all its nefarious traffic, is denied toleration by men and women wherever reason and truth and feeling prevail.

This question, "Shall America Go Back?" suggests an investigation of the progress of Prohibition. I am aware that from a technical standpoint the phrase may be open to criticism, because the very word Prohibition is a word of finality. But I must hold to the phrase all the same, and, if any grammatical rule is violated it must be regarded as a casualty in the interests of truth (as one of our homespun lecturers put it, "It may not be elegant, but it illustrates"). For we insist that the prohibition of intoxicating liquors in the United States has been, and is, progressive.

It has been progressive in its onsweep through the years. Review invites one's attention at a time like this.

Away back in the 1840s Abraham Lincoln wrote:

Of our political revolution of '76 we are all justly proud. In it was the germ which vegetated, and still is to grow and expand into the universal liberty of mankind.

Turn now to the temperance revolution. In it we shall find a stronger bondage broken, a viler slavery manumitted, a greater tyrant deposed; in it more of want supplied, more disease healed, more sorrow assuaged; by it no orphans starving, no widows weeping; by it none wounded in feeling, none injured in interest.

And when the victory shall be complete, when there shall be neither a slave nor a drunkard on the earth, how proud the title of that land which may truly claim to be the birthplace and the cradle of both these revolutions that shall have ended in that victory!

I feel Abraham Lincoln's spirit is here this afternoon.

Shall America Go Back?

But it has been a tedious, tortuous war of progression from Lincoln's time to this, a battle to the death, over and over again, with an enemy armed to the teeth with ample funds and cunning sophistries. But the blessing of an all-watchful and an all-conquering Jehovah hovered over the battlefield, the entreaties of mothers encamped around it, and the tears of the children baptized it. Through the long years public sentiment, created and nurtured by the noblest hearts and the most intellectual minds, has grown and ripened until at last the soil that gave birth to such immortals as Abraham Lincoln, Henry Ward Beecher, Charles Finney, John B. Gough, Dwight L. Moody and Frances Willard could no longer tolerate this monstrous wrong, and one glad morning America spread her starry banner to a new sun of liberty, and by constitutional Amendment repudiated the hitherto legalized iniquity.

Every step of the way has been contested. Ever since December, 1917, when Congress favorably acted upon the resolution recommending the Eighteenth Amendment, powerful and sleepless foes have sought to make it ineffective. Despite this organized and persistent opposition, one by one the States fell in line until but little over a year later the thirty-sixth state ratified the resolution, and so made possible the President's proclamation.

Supposed Case against Prohibition

Now our adversaries declare they have a case against Prohibition. In the indictment there are several counts.

First, they say: "Prohibition was surreptitiously secured."

They say that the Congressional resolution was passed and its ratification secured while "the boys" were overseas, and that but for this fact Prohibition never would have been possible. While this allegation, because of its repetition and the somewhat widespread belief it has been given, has been frequently and completely denied, permit me to cite the facts, with which many may not be familiar.

Who adopted Prohibition? The people themselves through their representatives in Congress and State Legislatures. In Congress 347 votes were cast for submitting the eighteenth Amendment to the State Legislatures for ratification and 148 against. In the forty-six states out of the forty-eight which ratified the Amendment 5,084 votes were cast in the State Legislatures for ratification and 1,263 against it. The total vote was seventy-nine percent for ratification and twenty one percent against.

You can impress the whole situation on your mind by remembering that Prohibition was "put over" by only forty six of the forty-eight states in the Union with only ninety-eight percent of the population and only ninety-nine and three-fourths percent of the area of the United States. To sum up, only two small states--Connecticut and Rhode Island--refuse to ratify. Prohibition could have been no surprise to the country, for thirty-three states were dry by state enactment and eighty-seven and eight-tenths percent of the area and sixty and seven-tenths percent of the population were under license law before the Eighteenth Amendment went into effect. How ridiculous to say that it was secured by surreptitious means!

Drink Always a Lawbreaker

The second count in this indictment is: "Prohibition does not prohibit."

It is rather strange that our enemies blow both hot and cold. We hear much about the drastic nature of the Stead Act. It seems to prohibit overmuch, and our friends say: "We would be satisfied if they would allow light wines and beers." Then with almost the same breath they say: "Prohibition does not prohibit." If it doesn't, then the "Wets" are well served. But they know it does, and that every time they slake their thirst with the forbidden beverage they are breaking the law. This, in the drinkers' realm, may not be looked upon as particularly bad, but then drink is always true to form, and in the days when it was legalized its devotees were the most flagrant breakers of the law in the land.

Drink will not be regulated. Its law-breaking proclivities are not new, but are as old as history. As a breaker of the law; be it laws of nature or laws of nations, laws of health or laws of home, laws of mind or laws of morals; the drink stands condemned, the red-handed criminal, the greatest law breaker in the land. So it is no new role for its apologists to assume when they cry: "Prohibition does not prohibit!"

That there are violations of the law all admit, but to cite that fact as an argument against the Prohibition Law is as futile as it would be to demand the cancellation of the whole decalogue because of repeated infraction of that law which is fundamental to all jurisprudence. It would be about as sensible to engage in an effort to expunge the Ten Commandments from the Book of God because of their non-fulfillment in the lives of men as it is to advance the theory that the Prohibition Law should be repealed because it does not prohibit.

Because the laws against arson, theft and murder are being violated, shall we abandon these laws and their penalties? Certainly not; and by the same token the Eighteenth Amendment and its supporting law must stand.

The True Test

The third count in this indictment is: "You cannot by law make men moral."

This statement cannot survive the acid test. Its reasoning is fallacious and its implications untrue.

I must remind our friends that the question is not simply and only one of morals. That phase of the matter, I admit, to Salvationists looms up with singular distinctness. We hold that it is positively wicked to take God's good grain, capable of sustaining the lives of multitudes who are now on the verge of starvation, and waste it, and not only so, but, in the process of waste, turn it into an unmitigated curse. No proprietary rights will absolve any from the moral obloquy of such conduct. To trade in that deceptive and destructive thing, apart from anything that statutory law may say, has long been regarded as of doubtful ethics. The beverage use of alcohol has proved with mathematical precision that it is a demoralizing and dehumanizing agent.

Oh, yes! It is a moral question, but not only so. It is also an economic question, a sociological question, a political question, a scientific question, and startlingly these days it has been demonstrated to be an international question. So it comes to pass that the economist, the scientist, the statesman, the sociologist and the manufacturer have all joined with the moralist in the enunciation of this law that was graven by the hand of God in the constitution of human life.

The statement that morality is divorced from law is not true. Moral conduct is the aim and end of law. That is the meaning of law. Its enactment and administration have good conduct for their objective, and while conduct may at times be governed by nobler considerations than fear of penalty, law is still universally recognized as necessary to the existence of well-ordered society.

When people say: "You can't legislate people into good morals," I reply: Into the whole fabric of our nation's law is woven the ethical element, and any law that violates a correct moral standard is foredoomed to dishonor and its repeal is certain. By this test the old liquor-license laws were tried and condemned and ultimately superseded, and I feel quite happy in the realization that the same searching trial will be applied to the new, for it will but reveal to the whole world the soundness of our present legislative position. Meanwhile depopulated prisons and rebuilt homes witness to the fallacy of this argument advanced against Prohibition.

Liberty Versus Anarchy

The fourth indictment is: "Prohibition invades personal liberty."

Into this supposed tower of refuge probably more of our opponents run than any other, and from its flimsy ramparts they fling the cry: "Prohibition invades our personal liberty by prescribing what we shall eat and what we shall drink; and we deny any man's right to prescribe our plum pudding or our exhilarating cup."

The principle which enters into the Prohibition Law is no more nor no less than that which is basic to the restraints of all law. No man objects to the denial of his liberty to steal; anyway, he doesn't object to the curtailment of his neighbor's liberty in this direction; therefore he should intelligently accept the application of this same principle to that house-breaking, home-destroying, child-abusing, business-wrecking thief, Alcohol.

Liberty, true liberty, is a priceless heritage, but no man's liberty comprehends a right to strike another down, not even if that other is his own child. In the exercise of society's right to protect itself, the nation came to an appraisal of the monstrous wrong that was perpetrated upon it by its permission of the drink traffic. Progress toward that evaluation was slow and tedious, but the final appraisal was correct; correct politically, correct economically, correct scientifically, correct socially and correct morally.

With the soul of the people awake to this solemn fact, there was no consistent course possible but for the nation to cleanse its hands forever from the cruel partnership that had dishonored it, and refuse longer to traffic in homes, in happiness, in health, in the very lives of its children. For this holy purpose our nation flung her starry pen across the Federal books and by strictly constitutional means wrote into the organic law of the land that which every officer and every citizen is pledged to support. In the name of all civilization I declare that there is no liberty apart from law. There is but one alternative, anarchy.

What about the enforcement of law?

That splendid American, the Honorable Charles E. Hughes, Secretary of State, says: "Everybody is ready to sustain the law he likes. That is not in the proper sense respect for-law and order. The test of respect for law is where the law is upheld even though it hurts."

Law must be, and it must be obeyed. Yet there are those who argue that breach of the Prohibition Law is excusable. Some say it is laudable, while others are defiant and make it their business in life to forward their sinister work of doing those things that the law prohibits. There are others that go still further; in their wild thirst for gain the lives of their victims count not, and murder is added to fraud, when they trade upon the weakness of their fellows and for fabulous prices sell deadly poison.

How sorrowful it is that opposition to Prohibition has united, as in a great dragnet, the good and the bad, so that the clean and respected citizen and the professional drink-exploiter are cogitating and cooperating together for the repeal of the Eighteenth Amendment! But "they shall not pass."

The Prohibition Law sprang from the soil and the soul. It germinated in remote and sacred places where mothers pray and fathers think. The country church, the country W.C.T.U., the country home and school took the lead, the West far in advance of the East. Long and wearisome has been the struggle. Shall those who fought and gained it ever go back? "Kansas," William Allen White says, "and states of her tradition and her kind would no more lose their forty years' fight for Prohibition than they would lose their four years' fight against slavery."

The Salvation Army and the Drink

I stand here today as a leader of a movement that, in its attitude toward the drink evil, has never known a hesitating moment. At the inception of The Salvation Army, over half a century ago, Prohibition was in its infancy and there was then no condemnation of moderate drinkers. A religious movement, with total abstinence as a condition of membership, was both novel and unpopular.

But the die was cast, for our Founder, my father, saw this was the curse that bound the poor man as with an iron chain to his poverty, and was both the forerunner and supporter of the worst crimes. Proscription was the only course, and that course, without a single exception, has been followed. Because of this we stand today the greatest temperance movement on the face of the earth. The Army has a right to voice its convictions and to testify to its experiences concerning intoxicating liquor, for its hands are clean!

It will be expected that I should say something as regards the immediate benefits of Prohibition as seen by The Salvation Army.

With whatever false reasoning some may delude themselves, our experience with all classes of society proves that with the ousting of the saloon, nine-tenths of the drunkenness of the country disappeared. Of all welfare workers none were in closer touch with those who were afflicted with this burning thirst than my faithful officers and people, and their uniform and irrefutable testimony clearly show that the chief source of former debaucheries is gone.

One of my principal officers, an unimpeachable witness, said to me only a few days ago: "In former days I usually had eight to ten drunken men in my meetings. Since Prohibition came I have only seen two men so conditioned in all my meetings throughout the country. Commander, something has happened!"

Yes, something has happened. The drink-sodden wretch, who formerly was the despair of law and almost the despair of the Gospel, is found in only rare instances. Those who are working for the repeal or the nullification of the Prohibition Amendment should solemnly ask themselves whether they are prepared again to expose their fellowmen to this terrible temptation and peril.

One of my officers in Kentucky tells of an old mountaineer who said to him: "Captain, six years ago I had no home, no possessions at all. For years I had been a

116

drunkard. My wife and children lived in poverty. Now I have built and paid for my house. I live in the hot summer months on my lot by the river." The mother was sitting in the rocking chair. A first class record was playing "Nearer, My God, to Thee." The old man said, "I owe it all to God and the men and women of God who put down the accursed drink." SHALL AMERICA GO BACK?

Testimony of Rescue Officers

The superintendent of our Slum Settlement Work tells me that applications for relief are reduced fifty percent. She says: "The majority we now relieve are widows. The families in the districts we visit are better fed, better clothed, and better housed. Another significant feature is the decrease of mortality among young children. It used to be a common thing for reports to reach us of babies that had fallen from fire escapes and infants that were smothered on account of drunken parents, but not one such report has reached us during the last year!"

Yes, something has happened. Our Women's Rescue Officers bear testimony to the effects of Prohibition upon the broken hearts of our city streets. These experienced workers cannot be deceived regarding the relation of strong drink or light wine to the social evil. They have a greatly simplified problem with the drink factor eliminated. Whereas in the past hundreds came to the refuge of our Homes as victims of wine-room or saloon-parlor seductions, today drink cases are rarely found, and from the different caliber of cases coming under our care it would seem that the baser forms of the monster's subtle designs cannot be sustained without the stimulus of intoxicating drink. SHALL AMERICA GO BACK?

Let me ask you to step back to the days of the wide swung doors of the saloon. Let me tear the film from the eyes of men who are blinded by mercenary gains and selfish appetite. Let me persuade mothers and fathers of every status of life for one brief moment to blot out every other consideration while here today we look to the handwriting on the wall of the nation, and read what is written there.

Such trembling strokes, such weak, shaky characters; such long spaces between words; words ill-formed, words ill-spelled, words ill-placed. Such simple little sentences, but vastly comprehensive--such faint impress, but never to be obliterated. Whose are the fingers that have wielded the trembling pen, the thin fingers, the misshapen fingers, the twisted fingers? Whose is the writing? Why it is the children's--the handwriting of the children, across the wall of the nation-- stretching from sea to sea!

Ah! You can hush every other voice of national and individual complaint; you may silence every other tongue, even those of mothers of destroyed sons and daughters, of wives of profligate husbands; but let the children speak--the little children, the wronged children, the crippled children, the abused children, the blind children, the imbecile children, the nameless children, the starved children, the deserted children, the beaten children, the dead children!

O my God, this army of little children! Let their weak voices, faint with oppression, cold and hunger, be heard!

Let their little faces, pinched by want of gladness, be heeded! Let their challenge--though made by small forms, too mighty for estimate--be reckoned with! Let their writing upon the wall of the nation--although traced by tiny fingers, as stupendous as eternity--be correctly interpreted and read, that the awful robbery of the lawful heritage of their little bodies, minds, and souls is laid at the brazen gate of Alcohol! SHALL AMERICA GO BACK?

The Challenge

I hear this challenge coming also as the voice of many waters from thousands of homes rehabilitated, from thousands of wastes reclaimed, from thousands of half-damned souls redeemed, from thousands of drunkards with manhood regained; from smoking flax and bruised reed, the chorus thrills on and on and on until it is caught up by ten thousand times ten thousand voices of faith and hope and love and liberty. Still on and on in vibrant tones it wings its way. Mothers in the cottage voice it, the sick in the hospital join in it, the children on the school bench lift it, the convict in the prison cell catches it, the striplings of new character in this new day shout it.

Still on and on the challenge rolls through garret and palace, over hill and through dale--onward and upward, higher and higher, until the dear ones in Glory catch the mighty sound and with all the redeemed, their faces aglow in the light of the Morning, join in as with a trumpet call that echoes along the everlasting hills.
SHALL AMERICA GO BACK?

ECB with former President Herbert Hoover in 1935

ECB with Aviatrix Amelia Erhart

ECB was awarded Gold Medal of National Institute of Social Sciences in 1933. Other Recipients were Newton Baker and Clifford W. Beers

ECB with Commisioners Edward J. Parker and Ernest I. Pugmirc

ECB with children at a 'slum outing'

ECB's home in Hartsdale, N.Y.

ECB in Japan in 1929

Photographs supplied by National Archives and Research Center, Alexandria, Virginia; George Scott Railton Heritage Centre, Toronto, Ontario and Commissioner John D. Waldron (R)

Freedom and Restraint
in the Use of Intoxicating Liquor

Editorial preface:

The following statements by the Commander-in-Chief of The Salvation Army in the United States were given a full page display in The New York Times. Let the liquor people and the opponents of the Eighteenth Amendment say what they will, here are the facts; and they are presented by one who has devoted a lifetime of study to the problem of inebriate manhood. Here are no gossamer theories; here are actual findings by those who sympathetically toil for the salvation of the drink slave.

Readers will admit that this is one of the most convincing and logical treatises of the Prohibition question that could be contained in the space required to print it. --- Editor

Do Drys Ever Amount to Anything?

"What total abstainer ever amounted to anything?" asks the sneering Wet.

Oh, just Abraham Lincoln, Thomas Edison, Admiral Perry, John D. Rockefeller, Robert E. Lee, Stonewall Jackson, Henry Ford, Whittier, Bryant,

Barnardo, William Booth, Nansen, Bernard Shaw,
Wilfred Grenfell, Gandhi, Lindbergh.

Of course, this isn't the entire list, but then this is
a small paper.

From The War Cry (New York), July 4, 1931.

Since my early girlhood I have lived in order to combat
the grave evils arising out of the liquor traffic. Hundreds
of times I have sung and prayed in the actual bars of the
public houses in London while the sale of beer and spirits
was proceeding. I have made my home in the underworld
and engaged in the pitiable industries of the sweatshop,
taken my place among the vendors of flowers and
matchboxes and with the street singers collecting their
pennies from the passersby.

My experience of this problem is thus at first hand and,
beginning in Great Britain, it has continued on the
Continent of Europe, in Canada and the Klondike, while, in
the United States I have completed twenty-five years of
service during which period I have been able to observe the
situation, both before and after the Eighteenth Amendment
came into force.

Opposition to Liquor Traffic

The Salvation Army stands wholly outside politics and
controversy and is well aware that its support of Prohibition
is not approved by many friendly newspapers and generous

121

contributors. With great respect to those who differ from us, we are bound, at whatever cost in popularity to say plainly that it would be impossible for us to carry on our work, except in direct opposition to the liquor traffic in all its forms.

In the use of beverages other than water, fermentation was never an essential, and today it is to an increasing extent eliminated. Tea, coffee, cocoa, served hot, with many cooling drinks, derived from fruits, have been developed as an alternative to wine, beer and spirits, and fulfill the legitimate purpose of what formerly was intoxicating liquor of varying strength.

There is an unanswerable case for abstinence. There are the vital statistics of insurance companies. There are the records of hospitals where patients, abstaining and non-abstaining, submit to surgical treatment. In major operations, it is admitted that a patient without alcohol in his system enjoys an advantage. There are strict rules imposed on athletes in training. But, more significant than all these, is the policy pursued by organized industry, in which, as the United States Steel Corporation has put it, "the last man hired, the first man fired" is "the man who drinks."

The subdivided processes essential to mass production, in which the strength of the human chain is no stronger than its least sober link, the increased speed and variety of locomotion at sea, in the air and along the highroad, the insistence on personal reliability in banks and offices, all this has necessitated in the United states an enrollment of abstinent workers. It means that the efficiency of the individual, when subjected to many varied tests, responds most readily and most reliably to a diet from which alcohol is excluded.

Difficulty of Restraint

Erring men and women have not found it possible to observe restraint in the use of alcohol, and, in all countries, at all times, the liquor interests, public and private, have seen to it that restraint is made as difficult as possible. The result is that wherever alcohol is used at all, it is widely abused.

As a result of an unexampled wave of prosperity, due in no small measure to Prohibition, many families, not long ago reckoned among the poor, have become comparatively and actually rich. It is thus a curious and ironical fact that in the very homes which owe much of their affluence directly to the economic results of the Eighteenth Amendment, there has been a tendency to discard the one restraint of which that affluence is the result.

The *nouveau* wets, as they go over the top into the barbed wire entanglements of what, in the United States, should be the no man's and no woman's land of a deliberate disobedience to the law, are like the soldiers at the outset of a war. They think a good deal more of the bands playing and the flags flying than of the casualties that come to The Salvation Army--the boy whose name is no longer mentioned, the girl whose name is known only to herself.

"Bravado" of the Cocktail

Drinking in wealthy homes did not begin with Prohibition. On the contrary, it was so usual before Prohibition as to arouse no comment. Today, that drinking, even where it continues is restricted. Many a cocktail is served and on special occasions only less as booze than as bravado. Many a glass has become little more than a gesture. The orgies described in cheap fiction, the bacchanals staged for the movies, the cheap jests and insulting cartoons which are showered on the drys, are merely symptoms that an ancient and world wide evil dies hard.

If, however, it had been the fact which we deny that Prohibition is a social failure, we would reply that what is here meant by the word society, and especially society in certain fashionable areas, does not constitute the nation but only a small proportion of the nation, at most one-tenth. The real question is what has happened to the nine-tenths and here the evidence of The Salvation Army is, we submit, direct and unchallengeable.

In New York before Prohibition, The Salvation Army would collect 1,200 to 1,300 drunkards in a single night and seek to reclaim them. Prohibition immediately reduced this gathering to 400, and the proportion of actually intoxicated persons on the day selected from nineteen out of twenty to no more than seven in all. In fact, this method of evangelism yielded so few results that we gave it up.

In The Chicago Daily News of April 1 and 2, 1929, interviews were published with our officers serving in that city. For No. 1 Industrial home, with 120 men, Sunday was

124

selected as a test day, because it immediately follows Saturday night. On one Sunday there were two drunks, and on the next, none at all. This record compares with 50 percent of drunks ten years ago and 25 percent of drunks four years ago.

In Chicago it happened that our Palace Hotel was subjected to an unforeseen and entirely impartial test. There had been a report of smallpox in the city and all the men in the hotel, about 500, were vaccinated, on the nights of January 10 and 11, by an independent physician. Not one of the men was found to be under the influence of liquor.

The women of American do not tolerate an inebriated manhood. It is no mere coincidence that the Eighteenth Amendment, prohibiting liquor, should have been historically simultaneous with the Nineteenth Amendment, giving the vote to women, and should have preceded by a few years only the proposed Twentieth Amendment, drafted to abolish child labor. These legislative enactments and proposals are, all of them, parts of a general movement toward the defense of domestic life against the destroying menace of selfishness in the environment.

The Great War was an explosion which shook not thrones alone but traditions and social restraints. By these disturbances women in the United States as well as men were affected and it is always in colleges that youth in its eagerness tries its experiments. Hence we have the statement that there has been more drinking among young people since Prohibition than formerly and this increase particularly affects girls.

So far as I am aware, there has never been any attempt to prove this by statistics or other definite evidence. It appears to be a case not of increased drinking but of greatly increased sensitiveness to the drinking that is taking place. At Oxford and Cambridge drink is served in the colleges as a matter of course, and no one thinks anything about it. The Salvationist notices that in the United States there has been not only reckless drinking but reckless thinking, reckless teaching and reckless preaching.

The public frequently is confronted by what seem to be appalling statistics. Nor is it realized that a big figure may represent what comparatively speaking is a small fact. Let us suppose that 10,000,000 persons in the United States spend no more than $1 a week on liquor. Even so, that aggregate expenditure would work out at $500,000,000, a very large number which taken by itself might be so presented as to suggest that the law had broken down. But what would be the truth of the matter? It would be that 100,000,000 people in the United states did not touch liquor from one year-end to another, and that even the 10,000,000 people were bone dry on six days a week.

It is under these circumstances that liquor takes a toll of $34 per annum for the individual and $3.25 per week for a household. It is true that rather more than a third of the expenditure is paid into the exchequer as taxation. It is a taxation that falls in the main on those who are least able to sustain it and, incidentally, it proves that high taxation even where it is strictly collected, does not solve the liquor question.

The liquor traffic can be handled in three ways: First, State ownership and control of the traffic; secondly, State restriction of the traffic; and thirdly, prohibition.

Over State ownership and control I need not waste many words. Under our Federal form of government in which forty-nine sovereign areas would have to be dealt with, the legal, constitutional and financial difficulties would be enormous, while politically such a scheme lies wholly outside the legislative possibilities. The idea that the consumption of liquor would be diminished by such a distributive network of selling places appears to be contrary to all the probabilities, and a legal glass of beer does just as much harm as an illegal glass.

The people who advocate such regulation have short memories. They do not seem to be aware that it was the failure of regulation throughout the United States that drove us into Prohibition. Nor is there any country in the world where regulation has solved the liquor problem. In the United States it was regulation which corrupted our politics, bribed our law courts and police and maintained our red-light areas.

The truth is that whatever restriction is placed by the law on the liquor traffic it will be the aim of the liquor traffic to rebel against it. No liquor traffic anywhere has kept faith with the law except in so far as the law is on the side of the liquor traffic.

The Salvation Army is wholly opposed to the policy of introducing light wines and beers sold under the law for consumption off the premises. That policy means the return of the saloon triumphant into our national life. Wherever beer is sold, there is the saloon, even if it be the back door of a rabbit hutch.

Let us suppose that 10,000 of such places were started in New York City. Does anybody suppose that such places, the very symbols of a criminal triumph over the forces of law and order, the rendezvous of bandits, bootleggers, racketeers and dishonest politicians, would be content with their profits on light wines and beers, or insistent on consumption off the premises?

The Law and the Rebel

There would be exactly the same forces organized to break down regulation that are today organized against Prohibition, and the idea that the rich man who likes his cocktail and his glass of whisky and his champagne is going to be content with lager beer and some scarcely alcoholic light wine as an alternative may be dismissed. He will say what he is saying today, that he has a right to drink what he likes and to get it where he can.

The idea that the provision of beer can ever be a cure for drunkenness is fantastic. More than half the alcohol consumed in the United States before Prohibition was in the form of beer. Most of the drunkenness was due to beer. On home brewing and distilling the view of The Salvation Army is equally emphatic. These are a defiance pointblank of the Eighteenth Amendment, which in plain terms forbids the citizen of the United States to manufacture alcoholic liquor. The idea that liquor has been or ever will be widely brewed by the individual family for its own exclusive use

128

may be dismissed. It is merely the revival of moonshine or the illicit still with which the United States has been long familiar.

The conclusion of The Salvation Army therefore has been in one sentence, that prohibition in the full sense of the word has been a major reason for the rapid advance of the United States to a foremost place among nations; that liquor not prohibited is a major reason for the retardation of a similar progress among other peoples of the world, and that if prohibition be attacked, whether by foreign nations or by certain of our own citizens, the reason is, in the main, a selfishness on the part of the individual or of the financial interest involved. In a sentence, the world is moving toward the view that liquor is a survival of the past; and, manifestly, Prohibition in the United States has come to stay and must be accepted as the law of the land.

Chapter Six
Seasonal Messages

Armistice Day Speech

Manuscript found in the Library of the School For Officers' Training, Suffern, NY. No indication of date or location of delivery.

Hearts have their memories as well as heads--unnumbered millions of hearts moved to a silence that is more eloquent than any speech, the silence of sacrificial sorrow, too deep for expression in words, a sorrow enabled by divine consolation, and mercifully glorified by the healing tenderness of time.

The silence embraces friend and foe in one brotherhood of reconciliation, surpassing frontiers of race and religion, and breathing everywhere a prayer to the Father of all, "Give peace in our time, O Lord, give peace. Bind up the bleeding wounds of cruel conflict, dry the tears that stain terror stricken faces, restore shattered homes, feed the victims of famine that shadows the battlefield. Give peace, O Lord, give peace."

Never in the long annals of human history has there been so passionate, so universal a will to peace as there is today. Nobody wants war. Everyone is horrified by the apocalyptic vision of what war means--the senseless devastation of cities, the strain and stress of finance, the deplorable loss of trade, the hideous wrong inflicted on mothers and their children, Nobody wants war.

There is no conceivable objective that justifies war. When the millions are slain, when the billions are spent, when the revolutions that accompany war have run their

131

dreadful course, when the treaties are signed as scraps of paper that war tears asunder, who has benefited?

The answer is, nobody!

We talk of war-profiteers. There are none. Everyone is impoverished in happiness when war sweeps civilization like as a locust-like scythe that reaps all harvests with poison-laden flame.

The world is moving rapidly along the highroad of progress. Manners and customs are changing. Communications--land, sea, air--are developing. We have to make a choice. Are we to understand one another better? Are we to be embittered by misunderstanding?

Understanding solves every problem. Know others as you know yourself and you cannot hate, you cannot intrigue, you cannot injure. Every blow at another becomes a bruise on your own countenance. God grant us understanding.

I speak today not for The Salvation Army alone. Every church--Protestant, Catholic, Jewish--is united behind my appeal for more understanding, less fault-finding, a deeply instructed sympathy.

Every church has learned by experience the secret of understanding, and it is a simple secret. Render service unto others, and you will soon understand established in justice and mercy, there will be no war, world without end.

Amen and Amen.

A Mountain Mother's Easter Morning

From The War Cry (New York), April 19, 1919.

Somewhere amid the pine-clad rockies of the far Northwest the sun lay its burning cheek upon the snowy pillow of the mountains. The shades of night already shadowed the little town, which clung like a child to the bosom of one of those quiet hills. A wayward child it was, much given to wild laughter, irresponsible indulgences and passions primitive and fierce, yet always at evening-time it seemed a tired child, weary of its ways and self, upon whom the overhanging mountains appeared to brood in maternal care and solicitude. The toils and soils of the day were over, and it was still too early for the recklessness and debauchery which defamed the majesty of the mountain night. Here one did not wonder at the audacity of him who called the twilight "God's hour."

Yet just at this hour a battle was raging--none the less terrible and grim because the battle-field was a human breast. Jim Carter had fought many battles with his hands, battles which had left their scars--usually, in Jim's case-- upon the other fellow. But now he met an adversary who was more than his match; an adversary whom no tricks of pugilist's art could catch off guard. Jim was caught, for the first time in his life, defenseless before the battering blows of his own conscience, to whose existence he had never given even a passing thought.

Though not yet twenty-five, Jim Carter was the acknowledged "bad man" of the mountain town. In a community infamous for its crime and lawlessness he was the hardest drinker, the most inveterate gambler, the wildest liver of them all. What impulse had brought him into the little shanty, half-store, half-dwelling, which served the local Salvationists for a meeting-house, he could never afterward remember. Perhaps curiosity; more likely the temptation to create a disturbance. But once inside a spell had fallen upon him against which he fumed and fought in vain.

It was not the eloquence of the appeal, nor the melody of the song, nor yet the fervency of the prayer which reached and smote Jim's long-hidden, hardened heart. The power of it, the pain of it, the plea of it all was that here spoke mother's faith, mother's Bible, mother's teachings. For fifteen years he had put a gulf between himself and his mother and her God, for he was one of the many prodigals to whom these sacred names are synonymous. He had deserted his mother, he had spurned her God, he had given himself over, body and soul, to all that was worst in himself. Yet here he was, writhing in impotent anguish against the force of good, just as if his foot on entering the meeting had touched off a hidden mine of violent explosives.

For two hours the struggle lasted, and when the climax came the strong man was weak. In sobbing jerks he poured forth his confession, revealing staggering depths and deeds to which the black years had been given. If the lurid story told by one so young, was a shock to the man of God kneeling by his side, his face bore no trace of such feeling, but rather the deeper became the great compassion of his eyes and the more tender and passionate his voice, reiterating the promise: "Though your sins be as scarlet, they shall be as white as snow; though they be red like crimson, they shall be as wool."

So the storm swept until the strength of both was far spent. Then came the moment when, utterly at an end of himself, the penitent soul threw his blackened life and blistered heart upon the mercy of God, and with the moment of surrender came the dawn of divine revelation. Things which before seemed far off and mystic were now the only realities, and when he flung out his two long arms in an attitude of appeal, he felt they touched the cross upon which hung his mother's eternal hope.

Trembling and shaken, but with the Sun of Righteousness changing his countenance, the man staggered to his feet.

"Thank you," he murmured, brokenly. "God was as good as your word and mother's. "And now, Captain," his voice gathering firmness, "I've got to get back to her. I don't belong here anymore."

Nor did he. Miracle that it was, the man already looked estranged from that bacchanalia of which he had been both boon companion and king.

With divine instinct, feeling that his work here was not yet finished, the Captain decided to stay by his stalwart convert and accompany him on his journey. The mother lived but a few miles away--by the railroad a two hours' journey--yet not a letter nor a visit had the boy spared her in all those fifteen years.

As if to register in the heavens Jim's first new day, the Easter sun crowned with gold the snow peaks of the great hills and showed to all men who looked up that whiteness and crowning go together.

The one train of the twenty-four hours stopped at a wayside station. Jim and the Captain were the only passengers to alight. The little depot was locked, and the two stood for a moment irresolute beside the trunk which Jim had insisted on bringing with him. He knew his own nature and was anxious to burn all his bridges--to leave no hostages in his city of destruction. "I don't belong there," he repeated, "and nothing belonging to me belongs there neither!"

The Captain volunteered to keep vigil till the expressman came, but this did not suit Jim.

"Captain, I feel, somehow, I'll need you. Stay by me, won't you, and see me through?"

"Then we'll carry the trunk between us," said the Captain, whose strong muscles were just as ready to lift a poor fellow's load as was his big, strong heart.

The two men and their burden made a pathetic picture, passing down the narrow street, which was little more than a mountain trail, each holding a handle of the trunk--the young man, whose handsome face and shabby clothes showed clearly the rapid travel of the misspent years; the other an erect figure, in smart Salvation Army uniform, of an older man, whose whole being bespoke whiteness and correctness of sterling character; the connecting-link, the trunk which told the story of the changed road.

Jim was visibly affected as they traversed the silent streets of his old home, empty now but thronged by his thoughts with a thousand memories of days gone by. There was the school-house, from which he had so often played truant; there was the church, where he had stood, holding mother's soft hand, while she joined in the singing. (He always said his mother's voice was the sweetest in the church, and he remembered well how he nearly pulled Sammy Stevens' ear off because he said it wasn't so.)

He had not passed that door since childhood, and he saw again the gray-haired pastor he had insulted and spurned; there also was the village inn, at which he had in bravado drained the first glass of his curse; but here at last was the best of all, the old home street, the street which, if he had traversed every street in the whole world, would be the only street dear to him! All other thoughts merged into the thought of mother.

Oh, how cruel he had been to her! How she had loved him! Did she still love him? Could she after fifteen years of his wicked neglect? Jim Slough had come over to sell the pig that wouldn't sell, and had told him his mother was very poor--in fact, that she was in want--but that she was always listening, watching and waiting for him. Could she forgive him? He never could forgive himself. What an awful thing sin was to make a fellow do what it had made him do! Father long dead, too! O mother!

Every cobblestone his feet stepped upon spoke some fond thing of her to the boy's penitent heart. The few forest trees left standing on the roadside, holding out their fresh, leafy arms, reminded him of how when a little fellow he used to run into her arms, stretched out that way on returning from school. The early breezes made the tree branches to wave becomingly, as though they would hasten him, and the moaning of the wind, coming over the

137

mountain, seemed to call: "Come, hurry; you may be too late!"

As they had advanced, the window panes of the cottages reflected the glory of the Easter morning, and the village awakened to a lovely Sabbath. As they came in sight of the plain little frame house, which had been the lode-star of their night's journey, a miner on his way to work stopped and stared in such sudden surprise that his dinner pail fell clattering to the ground.

"My God, if it ain't young Jim! Oh, thank heaven for this Easter morn! Boy, you're just in time! Your mother's took awful bad! My missus is with her. She says..."

But Jim heard no more. Dropping his end of the trunk he sprinted up the street, burst open the door of the little home, took the narrow, creaking stairs three at a time, calling with a note of agony in his voice:

"Mother, mother, it's Jim, come home! It's your wayward boy, Jim, come home!"

The little woman upon the bed was fast slipping out of the struggle called life, but the boy's voice would have called her back from the deepest grave; and so, with a tide of vitality which came alone from her heart, she opened wide her two arms, so long empty and hungering, and called back: "I am waiting for thee, as I have waited for fifteen years with my arms open!"

Then as she laid her pale cheek, cold with the chill of death, against the face of her son, she prayed:

"O God, I thank Thee that the pain and hunger of fifteen years has not been suffered all in vain! My prayers are answered and I may die while he is near!"

"God," called the loud voice of the returned prodigal, "by the love by which Thou hast blotted out my sins, Thou wilt spare her. She shall not die!"

When the Captain, who had followed with all haste possible, looked into the room the weary mother's heart was beating against the heart of her boy, and both were looking into the other's face, with eyes full of tears, with smiles shining through, which spanned a rainbow of promise from mother to son.

And in the street without a man still stood staring helplessly at a forgotten trunk and a spilled dinner pail, exclaiming over and over again:

"Just in time, by gosh! The Salvation Army do beat everything!"

Outside a rose covered cottage one can see, every sunny afternoon, a sweet little form, slightly bent, with silver-gray hair and two large soul-windows for eyes. She walks slowly around the small perennial garden, leaning upon the arm of a strong young man. On this particular day, when the heavens appeared to have forsaken every duty to caress the earth, if the one who saw had possessed as keen a capacity for hearing as the honey-suckle, he would have caught the words from the little mother's lips:

"I really do like her, Jim, for her own sweet self, and then all the more because she is a Salvationist. I confess that I was a little timid in case you fell in love with Ella Brooks, which would have meant your leaving The Salvation Army."

"Mother mine, never fear!" broke in the boy. The silver voice went on: "You know, Jim, I shall go into heaven thanking God for The Salvation Army, for it was these self-sacrificing people who gave me back my life and you!"

The Highest Compliment to Our Sex

A message from the General to Home League members, on Home League Sunday.

Found in the Library of The School For Officers' Training, Suffern, New York. No information on date of publication.

From time to time we catch the echo of an unworthy and cynical sneer at churches crowded with women. Religion, they say, is good enough for women.

I have always thanked the skeptic for that taunt. I welcome it as the highest compliment ever paid to my sex.

It IS the women who go to church. It IS mothers who pray for their husbands, sons and daughters.

For a woman deals with the innermost secrets of life itself. She handles the infant limbs of her child. She tends the sick father in his pain and weariness. She feeds the hungry. She soothes the sorrowful. In all ages, in all countries, she has fostered and safeguarded a faith in God. Women may at times have believed too much. But at least they have avoided the worse evil of believing too little. The women DO go to church and beyond! They can tread the *Via Dolorosa* of a faith that nothing in Heaven, nothing in Hell itself can shake from its foundations.

On the first Good Friday, when all the apostles had forsaken the crucified Christ and fled from the scene of His redeeming agony, it was the women who were last seen at the cross, watching Him there; and on the Morning of

141

Resurrection, when the night was still unlit by the first hint of the brightest dawn in history, the women were not afraid to risk the perils of those riotous streets and make their way, loyally and modestly and reverently, to the silent tomb.

Remembering these striking truths, I give thanks for the vast host of women who come to worship at the Army's Home League meetings. I know the great power that is in their hands to mold the lives of those around them, and I pray earnestly that they will more and more fulfil their high calling of prayer and faith and vision, looking well to the ways of their household by revealing to all therein the beauty of lives surrendered to Christ.

The Passover of Gladness

From The War Cry (New York), April 11, 1914.

I found the thought, or perhaps I should say the thought found me, in the pages of an old hymn book, whose fashion and phraseology both proclaimed it as belonging to the worship of other days. Such volumes always seem to be fraught with a sacredness second only to that attached to the Word of God, for on their leaves are inscribed lines which have upheld and inspired the saints of God in every variety of circumstance, crisis and calamity. Here is the language of penitence, the outpouring of praise, the assurance of present help in trial, the song of triumph in death, and that most resonant note--the promise of Resurrection. Such verses have wakened harmonies in the heart which all time cannot still, and have endeared themselves to every child of God and heir to the Kingdom.

But the hymn which suggested the words of my title was wholly unfamiliar to me, nor did I read it through. So deep and satisfying seemed this one line, that I looked no further, but lifted my heart in gratitude to God for the radiant message with which He had illumined my day--a message which, although the first buds of spring had not yet pushed their way up through the snow, wafted around me a fragrant breath of the new life of an Easter morning.

With the tragedy and peril which surrounded the first Passover we are all familiar. Sacred history has depicted for us that darkest of all Egyptian nights when the death angel brooded over the city, and only the blood-stained lintel saved the first-born of the home. In fancy we have seen the family gathered around the solemn feast, the children feeling, though not understanding, the momentous awe of the occasion, looking from the white, anxious face of the mother to the set, stern features of the father as in silence he leaned upon his staff. We have imagined their scarcely trusted joy in the hour of deliverance, their trembling hopes and fears as they remembered the sea which yet barred their way, their mingled uncertainty and confidence as they thought of the prospect of the Promised Land. It was a solemn, a reverent, an awe-inspiring feast, but even in its happiest aspect it could scarcely be said that there was anything so bright or so clear or so transforming as gladness about it.

But when we turn from the Passover under the Law to the Passover under Grace, there is no note of uncertainty, no feeling of apprehension, no tincture of fear to alloy the pure essence of hope. Easter is essentially the season of happiness; it is the joy-center of the Christian year.

In our Passover there is gladness for those who mourn. We come back from the open grave to face the empty chair, but the bitterest drop is taken from the cup, and a light shines in the blackness of bereaving gloom, irradiating such words as, "They that sow in tears shall reap in joy," or, "Now is Christ risen from the dead and become the first fruits of them that slept."

In our Passover there is gladness for those who toil. "There remaineth therefore a rest to the people of God." Not forever will nerves wrack, muscles strain, blood throb and limbs ache. The weariness of earth will one day be forgotten in the restoration and complete recuperation of heaven, of which I like to think not as a passive inertia but the tireless buoyancy of an immortal vitality.

In our Passover there is gladness for those who love their Lord, those who have learned to love Him here, have followed His love through the dimness and depression of mortal miasma, and look to see Him face to face in the perfection of Eternity's climate.

Christ our Passover is sacrificed for us.
I am the Resurrection and the Life.

And as we read the radiant assurances, like a cloak there falls from us the pall of winter doubts and dreariness. The time of the singing of birds has come; the warmth and light of an eternal Summer is wafted to us across the tide through which our Lord has gloriously passed, and through which He waits to bear us in like triumph. The sepulchre and the seal are broken, death's sting is eradicated, another and a better life is begun, and in its light and love and beauty all horror and hate and heaviness are lost to sight forever and forever, for this is: THE PASSOVER OF GLADNESS.

The Stable Door

A Christmas message.

From The War Cry (Toronto), Christmas issue 1897.

The first stars of that Eastern night shone out diamond-like midst the blackness of the firmament, as the two weary travelers halted at a wayside inn and made humble request for night shelter.

The city to which they journeyed was at last reached, but had it not been so it is doubtful whether another step could have been taken by the footsore ass or its anxious leader, who glanced continually at the pale, sweet face of his young wife, as she uncomplainingly endured the fatigue and suffering of that exceedingly trying and uneven journey. "No room in the inn" was the gruff and impatient reply, for it was not the first refusal given that night; the little town of Bethlehem being over-crowded by strangers pouring into its quiet precincts to pay their registration dues. Whether it was a sense of compassion awakened by the patient face of the tired woman, or whether it was anxiety to ensure the small fee which the stable-shelter could exact, which permitted Mary and Joseph to house with the oxen.

I am not prepared to say, but I fancy I see her alight from the saddled ass, and with an expression of anxious wonderment enter "the stable door."

A stable, contemptible in its meanness, degrading in its associations, forlorn in its appearance! By its rudeness of

146

structure and separation from human inhabitants suggesting a significance of birthplace for One who was to become an outcast "despised and rejected of men."

How prophetic is its rude interior! What symbols of momentous and eternal happenings are its misshapen fittings!

The gnarled and knotted beams supporting the uneven roof throw, in their distorted shadows, emblems that upon their like rugged forms was to be stretched this night's Gift in the agonizing throes of the death of Jesus and the birth of a world's Redeemer. The unkempt shepherds hastening from the great flocks upon Bethlehem hills are His first worshipers, significant of how the first place was ever given in the God-nature of Christ and the compassion of Jesus to the most lowly, the most poor and the most needy.

Dare we not discover in the flinty composition of floors and walls (the stable being partially a cave cut out of rock) the distant clatter of falling flints with which in manhood years they stone Him? And is not the whole of His first dark, inhospitable abode but a preliminary declaration of the whole life that is to follow, missioning the darker and poorer homes of sin and sorrow?

As I look upon this rough structure fain would I direct the whole world not to the star that guided the wise men from the East, not to the orchestra of angelic throng who carolled "good-will on earth," not to the vacant place in the Kingdom of Light, but to the stable. In this dark, unimportant byway shelter I find as hidden treasures lessons of vastest import, which it must ever repay our being at some trouble, if needs be, to discover amid the unpretentiousness of their disguise.

First, I find from this stable scene that one can never tell what great events are in small beginnings--how that often those things which at their starting may appear the most insignificant hold issues of the greatest possibility either for good or evil.

The amazed shepherds needed all the help that vision and voicing of angelic choir singing His birth could render, to enable them to believe that the tiny infant of the maiden-mother, wrapped in coarse linen, pillowed in an uncouth manger between ox and ass, was any other than an ordinary child, of ordinary parentage, born in unfortunate circumstances, to begin and conclude life in unrenowned obscurity.

It would have been just as difficult to imagine that the babe, under sentence of death, taken from the bulrush cot by the daughter of Pharaoh, was destined to lead a nation from bondage and establish the law for the ages. Just as impossible a task for a people of another and later age to believe that in a small back room of a low German saloon was born Martin Luther, the mightiest of the world's reformers, whose voice of thunder was to rock a world's foundation of unbelief, and lay low the bulwarks of a universal delusion.

So it is just as impossible to know what lies in our cots!

Mother, as you rock your babe to and fro, soothing it with gentle murmur, or hushing it by lullaby, in your arms of love you clasp infinite possibilities, everlasting consequences, eternities of blessing or woe. So watch your treasures as the holy mother watched her first-born. It is not of so much account whether the swaddling clothes be composed of coarse linen or fine cambric, the pillow of

148

straw or down, but eternal importance is incased in the early aspirations and inspirations infused into infant hearts lending color and light for lifelong and eternal reflections, as the sun gives the violet its hue and the buttercup its gold even before its budding.

Give one-half the virtuous endeavor and holy care to the cradles, nurseries and schoolrooms of our world which today is thrown out in ministerial effort for deliverance from sin and from crime in all their grown and monstrous proportions, and coming generations will show three parts of the evil of the universe thrown overboard, and the tramp of the advancing good will make the teeth of remaining iniquity to chatter.

Don't wait until your child is of years before you introduce it to virtue. As soon as the natural eye can detect the shining of a star in the midnight sky, speak to it as to what is beyond. The stars will serve well to show the awakening intelligence how virtue and truth will shine all the brighter because of the black darkness of a world's sorrow and sin.

Then there are our cradle opportunities often coming to us so marked with poverty, and so closely surrounded by disadvantages, that in their infinitesimal proportions it is easy to treat them with indifference, lose sight of or abuse them. Yet it is but the crowd of these beginnings which go to make up life, and tiny as they seem, in reality they are great infinities, characterizing the life, death and eternity of a soul. Surely nothing can be less than a magnitude that is an attribute to a soul's eternal gain or eternal loss!

If virtue, no matter how small at its outsetting, or humble its birthplace, can grow so rapidly and travel so fast; then the value set upon its smallest and earliest expressions must be infinite.

Your opportunities for upholding the truth may not give you a bigger chance than that of a village street corner, or of pointing a soul to heaven by a word at the kitchen back door, or of telling the children of Jesus before you kiss them all around for the night, or a prayer for God's blessing on a comrade whose burden is heavy to bear.

All small, and even if well used scarcely worthy of mention, yet not smaller than the look which brought Peter to repentance, transforming the conquered to the conqueror. Not more simple than the faltering words of the little servant lass leading to the healing of Naaman the leper.

Not more insignificant to a world's bedimmed eye than that humble nurse-girl's endeavors to bless the little boy of eight who, when in his future a nation crowned him with honor and blessing, he crowned her before the nation as the instrument of his salvation. What a returning of "the bread upon the waters"--how more than worth the waiting "of many days!" 'Twas Lord Shaftesbury's nurse-girl's first chance of serving God. It was but a cradle opportunity, but she used it so faithfully that God made her "a mother in Israel" and blessed her name among women.

Secondly, I learn from the uncouth cot which forms earth's first resting place for our Lord and King, that unfitting and even unseemly circumstances can be made to render eternal profit to ourselves, and blessing and uplifting to others. You only want to put Jesus into them.

Could there be more ungainsayable proof that adversity has no power to hinder the purposes which God has hidden in the different happenings of our lives? What potency had poverty or degradation, shame or ignominy, to detract from the future of the Christ-heart whose first breaths were drawn without the presence of a luxury and hardly the forthcoming of a necessity. All that could best have been done without was present; all that the occasion claimed was absent.

The clattering of tongues without, the lowing of oxen within, the irregular and ill-sheltered walls through which the chill damp of the Eastern night had no difficulty in penetrating the crackling, shifting, prickly straw, so unsuitable to be the resting place of any but the beasts of the field; the garish publicity of the unlocked door; not one inconvenience was wanting, nor discomfort lacking around the most sensitive and delicate of maiden dispositions.

That stable was but the forerunner of the crowd of adverse circumstances which thronged around His life. They pressed again upon Him in His infant days, in the hurried midnight flight into Egypt from an intent murderer; they centered in the constant privation and monotonous occupation of the carpenter's daily toil; they fastened the continual discomfort and sorrow of homelessness upon one who had not where to lay His head; they clamored loudly after Him in the starvation of the wilderness, in the grief and agony of His last days upon earth.

But all these forces of evil held no power to impede the progress of a world's benefactor. The darkness, pain and sorrow of all these happenings attempting to eclipse the first rays of light divine only intensified its brightness, until its radiance was recognized by the whole world's millions as Love, Light and Life.

I see by this that adverse circumstances can never be blamed for an unsatisfactory state of the soul. They can only hinder in so far as you will let them do so, for God purposes that our seasons of adversity should be of eternal blessing. The grace of Jesus carried into trial makes it the school in which all must master before they can attain their heavenly degree; lessons which alone can fit us to stand where angels praise and martyrs sing.

How we love to think about them--those gone on before. How patiently they endured the pain, how lovingly they treated those that hated them, how earnestly they prayed for those that murdered them, how they shone when the darkest shadow fell. Now none stand nearer the Master than this triumphant throng. Their reward glistens in crown, in robe, in song.

Maybe your mother is among them. It was the fire of loss of children, of husband, or of all, which purified the gold, or it was the slow, cruel process of hard daily toil and momentary cross-bearing that trimmed the lamp, or the life-long effort to do something for Jesus despite a weak, crippled body that fitted the saint.

It has always been so. As there are some crops only ripened through the seemingly destructive processes of frost and rain, so there are many graces which can only be brought to maturity by the stern nurturers of hardship and affliction, or the fires of sorrow and persecution.

But the God of the saints who have gone on before is your God, and will see you through all the trials and tribulations. Do not be discouraged. Look up, and press on. Then, if things should go hardly with you, if trials should come in like a flood, if the burden is heavy to carry and the sky dark over your head, do not look for an easier path; do not say, as I have known so many, that you are not where God wants you, and seek for another to carry your cross.

Remember all that the road from the manger to Calvary brought to Jesus and to a poor, lost world, making forever circumstances, suffering, hardness and privation, death, and even the grave, but a golden staircase lifting to the highest development of character--the best experience of soul and at last to the bosom of God. Trial cannot hurt you, it can only bless you. So follow hard after Jesus, for there is laid up for the cross-bearers a crown in Glory.

Thirdly, I find that no words could express or mind well imagine the difference there was made in the stable by Jesus being there.

No comparison could be drawn between the manger holding the scanty allowance of food, for the over-taxed and exhausted ox, and the manger cradling its heavenly burden overshone by the light of a mother's first love and enhanced by a halo, telling of glory forsaken for a greater glory yet to come.

Might we not say that that gloomy and misshapen place of shelter held richer treasure than heaven itself contained? Had not the door of the world of light opened to let pass out that which through an open stable door to the woe of earth passed in? Did not angelic host crowding battlements of glory and thronging shining portals find more of heaven housed within that rude cattle shed than was to be found amidst all the grandeur of Jewish temple, that stupendous pile of pomp and magnificence, the pride of Jerusalem?

153

Yes, I see the stable grander than the temple; its cramped space further-reaching than the corridors, its manger higher than the throne.

All the light come -
All the glory brought -
All the difference made -
by Jesus being there!

Jesus on straw--taking out all the stiffness for saints who have no better bed to lie on. Jesus wrapped in coarse linen--making it of no matter of what poor stuff your coat is, but only of importance how rich in grace you are. Jesus in the dark--lighting a candle to brighten every shadow across the road from stable, store, carpenter's shop, fisherman's hut, widow's cottage, toiling loom and earth's saddest places, to heaven.

Jesus in a stable--making it happy and bright, and filling it with blessing for tired shepherds and seeking worshipers, so that He could come into your house and transform the gloom, and take out the cold, and light up the dark and dry the tears, and save from wrong.

It was Jesus made all the difference!

Here is a home. I know its carpets are threadbare, and its table may be scantily spread, but it is not that which makes the trouble. The father has a bad temper; he professes to be a Christian, but is not converted; he keeps a good appearance and talks pleasantly to people with whom he transacts business at the office, but at home he is full of impatient complaint. He storms because his slippers

154

are lost, the meat is either cooked too much or too little; he declares the place is a bedlam for the noise of the children.

The mother always says her head aches. She means her heart does, because something goes wrong in every day. All life is a weary drag. There is competing with the neighbors, getting the children to school, soothing the sickly baby; and so with the tedious round of a purposeless life time rebounds into eternity.

One night the father gets converted. His face is brighter than it has ever been seen. The children are told of the change, the Bible is dusted and brought out, the mother breaks down in prayer as she says: "O Lord, forgive my sins, and save me too!"

The children cry, and the father, with unusual hoarseness, pronounces the benediction, husband and wife kiss each other, children throw their arms around their parents' necks, and though there are many tears, it is "Peace on earth, good-will toward men."

Jesus has come in! Tradesmen, office hands, neighbors and schoolmates all know well the difference and say, "Salvation has come to that home," throwing sunbeams from within as from the stable, lifting first prayers as with the shepherds, offering incense and myrrh of holy living as with the wise men. Have Jesus in your home.

Lastly, and perhaps that which the most strongly appeals to my heart as I look on this sacred hostelry of Bethlehem, is the open door; open in the darkness of an Eastern night to a weary traveler; open to the hungry gaze of crowding and eager spectators; open, awaiting the coming of worshipers from the East, the North, the South and the West--for since that hour of heavenly carol and birth of

Peace, pilgrims from all parts of the universe have made their way in spirit and truth to the open "stable door."

No armed soldiers guarded the entrance, no double-barred gateway protected his gentleness, no silken-fringed curtain hid the countenance. It was just across an outer courtyard through a flung-open door, two paces over a rude, uncarpeted floor, and one was close beside Him, could kneel before and look upon Him, could place the offering of gold or precious stone upon the infant lap. I see the coming Redeemer of the world easy to find, easy to behold, easy to reach.

Pass the tidings through all the nations of the earth, an "open door" to Jesus.

I knew a gentleman who tried to get an interview with the late Queen of England. The columns of this paper would not hold the names of all the magnates who had to be approached, the lengthy letters that were written, the persistent and elaborate explanation of the character of the business that was despatched, the knots of red tape that were tied and retied, and the whole army of endeavors ending in the gentleman being introduced to a noble nobody!

But here is Jesus, the King of all kingdoms, the Prince of all nations, the Lord of all honor, and the song which first proclaimed His royal presence in the "Unto you is born," carols a world-wide invitation to all who will to pass straight in, straight in.

You need not wait to change your apparel, you need not be anxious as to the obeisance with which you approach Him, you need not strive to assume the attitude of any better person than the one you are, you can pass just as you are, straight in to Jesus--Jesus the Christ.

Do the troubled of earth's sorrowing paths know the door is open? Oh, what a dreary time the past has been carrying your bereavement all alone! God meant the taking of the bread-winner to do for you what it did to the widow of Nain--bring you in touch with Jesus. The promise made at the grave was in answer to His Spirit, when you said with God's help you would make straight for the port into which the treasured loved one had gone. But love of the world and sin pressed you further from heaven, putting a bitterness into every tear dropped since that grave was opened; just the bitterness which Jesus and His salvation would have taken out.

Now the best of your days are gone. It looks dark behind and darker before. You wish you were a Christian. You see how much better it would have been to love and to serve God! You feel so helpless. You are hedged in by evil influences, worldly associations and cruel circumstances. Yet does not this very hour, a guiding star shining in the darkness of your sky, throw its rays around an open door to Jesus?

I persuade you to do at once what the shepherds did--go straight in, tell Him all the wrong of your past, all the sorrow of your heart, all the failings and defeats which crowd your experience. His love will receive you! His blood will cleanse you! His grace will be all-sufficient for you!

No tears that He will not wipe, no burdens that He will not carry, no sorrows that He will not share, no weariness that He will not relieve.

157

Oh, blessed be God! And blessed be heaven! And how much more blessed is earth for an open door to Jesus!

Open to the blasphemer whose lips are filled with vile utterances!

Open to the backslider, whose feet are torn with sad wanderings! Open to the worldling whose soul is polluted with vanity! Open to the young and open to the old, open to the rich and open to the poor. None need go hungry, none need go sad, none need perish! Goodwill toward men, peace on earth and joy in heaven.

Let every angel sing it! Let every bell peal it! Let the ransomed shout it! Let all the hosts of all worlds prove it!

Keep the Bible to the Front

The General asks for a continuation of the Bible Week spirit.

From The War Cry (London), April 27, 1937.

The institution of an annual Bible Week cannot but bring great blessing and spiritual enlightenment, and I am delighted to hear of the way in which in very many corps special efforts were last week made to call attention to God's word.

I sincerely trust that this interest will not be allowed to die. One of the dangers of a special "week" devoted to any particular aspect of our work and life is the possibility of our feeling that with the close of the week we can legitimately turn our attention to other things, having done our duty toward the special claim.

In order to guard against this possibility and to make Bible Week of great value, I am asking officers and soldiers to keep the Bible where it ought to be in their personal lives and their activities on behalf of others.

The Bible is the Book of all books. Its enemies have searched high and low for every argument that might be used to refute its statements, to destroy its teaching and deny its miracles. Infidel scientists have marshalled against the Bible, the astronomer's telescope, the explorer's fathoming-rod and the geologist's hammer. But against the assaults of cynics, of critics, or skeptics, the Bible stands unaltered, immovable and unshaken.

159

Despotism has thundered forth edicts against the Bible. Fires have consumed it. The blood of countless martyrs has stained its pages. But despite all persecution, all suppression, all destruction, the Bible triumphs, a perpetual and ever more victorious resurrection from the tombs built around its living words by the unbelief and sin of man. The Book is God's and He guards it.

No power can tear down in the heart of countless millions that altar to which they bring their griefs, their sins and their perplexities, and find inscribed thereon the assurance of a Savior's love, pardon and consolation.

The Bible is everywhere. It is found within the prophet's mantle, the fisherman's coat, the shepherd's smock, the housewife's apron. It has its place on the judge's bench, in the soldier's knapsack, on the merchant's desk, in the salesman's suitcase, the sailor's bunk and the schoolgirl's satchel.

When I see that there is no spot, or condition, or circumstance, or individual for which the Bible is not suited, I am convinced that only God could have written a book so marvelous.

The Salvation Army is a mission of the poor to the poor; to the desolated and forgotten masses, and amid the indescribable miseries of the underworld, the teaching of this Book has been the one undimmed lamp. Multitudinous have been the hands of the poor who have taken the Bible as their sword of defense against the hardships of life, and who have clasped it to their hearts as the one help for the helpless at the hour of death.

The Bible is indispensable to the equipment of the Salvationist. It provides the Christian soldier with the daily ration on which depend his faith, his courage, his character. It is the armory wherein he finds the weapons of attack and defense, by which he wages his holy war against whatever destroys the happiness and degrades the life of others.

A Salvation Army, deprived of the Scriptures, would be an Army demobilized by the enemy of souls and held helpless within the entanglements of a secular and selfish world.

For myself, you may take from me all that life holds dear, but you shall not take away my Bible. I pray that this shall be the sincere conviction of all my comrades in The Salvation Army.

Time

A New Years message.

*From the Library of the School for Officers'
Training, Suffern, New York, dated December 1938.
No further information on date of publication.*

The Old Year is dying; a New Year is coming to birth;
and in squares and boulevards crowds gather and await the
twelve slow and resonant strokes of the inexorable hammer
that commands farewell as the Present surrenders to the
claim of the Past. Millions sing the Auld Lang Syne of
momentary remembrance, and salute, too often with
thoughtless cheers, the Future, which so full of grave
significance, is hidden from human vision and known only
to the providence of God.

Let the troublous time that passes--past, present and
future--be merged into Eternity, which is the same
yesterday, today and forever, wherein the plan of life is
visualized, not in broken parts but as a whole, and wherein
too is witnessed the gradual victory of the King of kings
and Lord of lords over all that disputes His authority or sets
aside His Gospel as of no account.

For the Salvationist this midnight hour is one of
dedication to further acceptance of responsibility. It is to
be spent within the impregnable watchtower of faith, where
God commands the garrison of witness to His love and
mercy and righteousness--that witness which is kindled as

a beacon of peace and justice among nations and among classes within nations.

In the varied and far-reaching realms of industry, commerce and finance this season of the year is observed with a special sense of what is due to the individual firm and to society as a whole. The New year is a festival of accountancy, when profits and losses are accurately ascertained, and assets and liabilities are set forth plainly in a balance sheet that determines whether there is solvency or insolvency, progress or retrogression.

The auditor of the Christian's accounts is Omniscience, and a false balance is abomination unto the Lord, whose desire is truth in the inward parts. Let us begin the year of grace at the Throne of Grace, giving glad glory to God for many outstanding triumphs of His love and power, and being thereby encouraged to confess wherein we have failed to claim a full measure of His all-conquering might. Let us seek forgiveness from Him Who is faithful and just to forgive, and rise up stronger in that all-sufficiency which is ours by promise and inheritance in Christ.

It is over one hundred years since the author Bulwer-Lytton added a proverb to our language. "Time," he said, "is money." We spend time and we save time, and we give time and we use time and we waste time, as we spend and save and give and use and waste money. It is of time that, at this midnight hour between two years, we have to give an account.

The employer is under no illusions as to the value of time. Countless millions of workers are called upon daily to punch the clock, and they lose pay if they are late.

Efficiency in management means the full use of the worker's full time.

The service of Christ is not compulsion. It is perfect freedom. But how much more of a sacred obligation is the time that He bought by His precious blood shed on Calvary, than the time for which the employer pays at so much an hour! The time of a follower of Christ is the most valuable time in the world.

The airplane roars through the air with the speed of an eagle. Trains are streamlined in order that they may add a few miles an hour to their record. Ocean liners are built to cross the Atlantic in four days. What invention, what expenditure, what heroism and effort are devoted to save a few hours and even minutes of a passenger's time! Yet too often people rush through clouds and tunnels and over oceans in order to be dull and listless in a hotel, where they do not know from minute to minute how to pass the time which in their mad hurry they have saved. How careful should be the use of the time of a child of God! How vital it may become with duty accomplished and ends that are written in the eternal records, and how disastrous if wasted!

Jesus impresses on us the infinite value of the time for which He paid so high a price on Calvary. He warns us against frittering away those opportunities of essential service which belong to Him as Redeemer by right of redemption, reminding us that, "The night cometh, when no man can work." For every idle word, He says, we must give an account. Let us observe, then, this season of accounting as in His sight, remembering that at this point of life's journey God hath no greater gift for us than the year ahead, and that this gift is conferred but one day at a time; there is no signpost to denote where the road for you or for me will end.

The Apostle Paul bade both the Ephesians and the Colossian Christians to be careful of "redeeming the time." That is what we have to watch for especially in this new age.

Psychologists tell us that as a rule we use only one-tenth of our brains. During the World War it was amazing to observe what courage, initiative and intelligence developed, under the stress and strain of the trenches, in the most unlikely men, whose lives had formerly been lethargic, ignorant, frivolous. They became what they might have been in earlier years if similar demands had been made upon them, the nearer to death, the more abundant the life.

On the battlefields of God the wholehearted Christian soldier mobilizes those of his faculties which have oft-times lain fallow. Herein is discovered one of the secrets of The Salvation Army's power in the world: uneducated, untrained men have become mighty servants of God because they not only consecrated all their strength and talents to be divinely quickened, but exercised them at full stretch for the Kingdom. Unsuspected reserves of ability and character have been let loose.

The soldier of Christ is never too young and never too old to volunteer for service under the flag of the Gospel. His youth and his experience are alike needed in the elaborate and powerfully equipped corps to which he is assigned.

God said, "I will magnify Joshua." It is true to this day that the man who is wholly given to God becomes magnified; he grows into the measure of the stature of the fullness of Christ, who, being Son of God, dwelt among us as Son of Man.

Children of God should watch most carefully and pray most earnestly that they do not waste time or throw it away. Time is lost by the careless; time is lost by the selfish; time is lost by the vicious. It is not to be wondered at that sometimes we are awakened to the thought that the world is behind the times, that in this age of enlightenment and education and Christian teaching evils continue which long ago were exposed to public abhorrence, that systems are enforced which earlier were declared by public opinion to be obsolete.

"Now is the day of salvation" is the clarion call of God, whose suns and planets in their celestial courses meet the demand of time to the second. Too often has man answered, "Not now, some other day," and with the acceptance of the Gospel in sad arrear what wonder is it if an unhappy civilization, unsatisfied by material enjoyment and enraged by material privation, rushes into wars and revolutions?

It is time lost by others as well as by himself that the Christian is called upon to redeem. The harvest is plenteous, the laborers are few, and for those laborers time has to be overtime--work has to be overwork--and grace has to be beyond all human reckoning, a sufficiency for every need and strength made perfect in every weakness.

Chapter Seven
Songs and Poems

Selections from "Songs of the Evangel"

Published by Salvationist Publishing and Supplies, London (1937), containing 29 of her songs, some with the stories of how they were written.

We have included five of the best loved songs from this collection:

> *Fling Wide the Gates*
> *I Bring Thee All*
> *The Wounds of Christ*
> *And Yet He Will*
> *O Save Me, Dear Lord*

Fling Wide the Gates!

After twenty-five long years, I seldom can look upon our Founder's picture but through a mist of tears. The glories of his character, the immensity of his vision, the largeness of his faith in God for man, and the unspeakable tenderness of his father heart; all these are portrayed in his face. What his passing meant to suffering, sinning humanity the world may know; but the unutterable emptiness of life without him to me, none can understand! It was in the early months following his promotion to the skies that one dark, sad day I shut myself in alone with that picture in all the poignant realization of my loss. With straining eyes I strove to follow that magnificent spirit as it soared toward a better and brighter world. Suddenly there seemed to throb around me the music of celestial spheres in a tumult of welcome and reward. I fancied I could see my father at his finest and best, stepping forward to meet on the threshold of Glory the One he had loved so long and served so faithfully, while through the gates I caught a glimpse of the throng, ten thousand times ten thousand, passing up the steps of light--the redeemed who through my father's life of sacrifice and toil had gone before him. And in the confidence of that vision there sang this paean through my soul.

Fling Wide the Gates

Andante maestoso M. ♩ = 44 (or ♩ = 88)

1. Fling wide the Gates! I hear the an - gels sing - ing;
2. Fling wide the Gates! A life of war - fare end - ed!
3. Fling wide the Gates! Thro' Christ his work ac - com - plished;
4. Fling wide the Gates! With hearts of glo - ry bril - liant;

Fling wide the Gates! I hear bright mu - sic ring - ing;
Fling wide the Gates! A sol - dier brave as - cen - ded;
Fling wide the Gates! His toils for oth - ers fin - ished;
Fling wide the Gates! His en - try made a - bun - dant;

A war - rior soul from this poor world is wing - ing,
Life's bat - tle won, the cause of Christ de - fen - ded,
Laid down the sword, the cross for crown re - lin - quished,
Tri - um - phant soul, with es - cort host re - splen - dent,

T'ward the glo - ry of the Gol - den Strand. (the Gol - den Strand.)
More than con-qu'ror thro' the pow'r of God. (the pow'r of God.)
Hal - le - lu - jahs fill the earth and sky. (the earth and sky.)
Stands be - fore the ho - ly throne of God. (the throne of God.)

Toil and fear, a sol - dier's spear, Left be - hind the grave,
With a bound at trum - pet sound, From its bond of clay,
Strug - gling hard, and bat - tle - scarred, Makes the Gol - den Shore,
Burn - ing brand in ev - 'ry land Blazed a ho - ly trail,

170

Proved His pow'r to save.
Winged His soul a - way.
Greets those gone be - fore.
Heav'n and earth do hail.

Hear the crown'd the an - them swell, 'Conqu'ror ov - er death and hell.' (and hell.')

I Bring Thee All

Out of the purple shadows of the Borderland God had called me back to life and service. I remember something of those days during which, semi-conscious, I hovered between two worlds. I had suffered so terribly and so long, and was broken in every fibre of my being. But as my blood quickened, as my eyes began to clear, and the fragrance of the lovely Spring breathed upon me through the open window, the precious reality of life was verified to me. Again to speak for Him, again to live for Him, again to win lost souls for Him! The pricelessness of the treasure overwhelmed me! With fingers that trembled I made my first effort upon the strings of my beloved harp, and the new consecration of my every faculty crystallized in the song: "I Bring Thee All."

I Bring Thee All

Andante con espress. M. ♩ - 56

1. Fa - ther of love, of jus - tice and of mer - cy,
2. O Thou, of Whom the heav'ns are but a sym - bol,
3. O Man of Sor - rows, pray - ing in the Gar - den,

Thou art the dawn, the star at ev - en - tide;
Be Thou the sun that draws my heart to Thee;
Thy sweat as blood falls down up - on the ground.

Show Thou Thy face, And light my way to Cal - v'ry,
Be Thou the light the stars at night do kin - dle,
In that dark a - go - ny my sins are par - doned;

There all my sins in Thee to hide. I bring Thee
Thy love is more than all to me. I bring Thee
My so - lace in Thy grief is found. I bring Thee

all my sins,— None can for - give but Thee.
all my heart,— None do I love like Thee.
all my tears,— None can con - sole like Thee.

173

CHORUS

I bring Thee all, I bring Thee all;

Oh, give Thy - self to me, I bring Thee all.

The Wounds of Christ

Returning to my quarters late one November evening, after battling with cold, sleet and misery, dressed in rags that I might get nearer to the hearts and lives of the poorest of those with whom I mingled in the slums of London, I vainly struggled to banish from my mind and pitying heart the awful scenes I had looked upon. Men, women and children with broken lives, broken hearts and broken characters; hopeless and helpless, trapped like animals at bay. One picture I could not banish: the beautiful face and golden head of the little fifteen-year-old mother, appearing in the filthy, dark, box-like room as a jewel amid ruins; the fast and bitter tears falling on the human mite dead in her arms; the despair in the frightened blue eyes as she said: "Look, there is no place for us in life, or in death; no place for the baby, or for me. Where can I hide the baby? Where can I hide myself?" One o'clock the following morning I wrote the song which has winged its way all around the world:

The wounds of Christ are open,
 Sinner, they were made for thee;
The wounds of Christ are open,
 There for refuge flee.

175

The Wounds of Christ

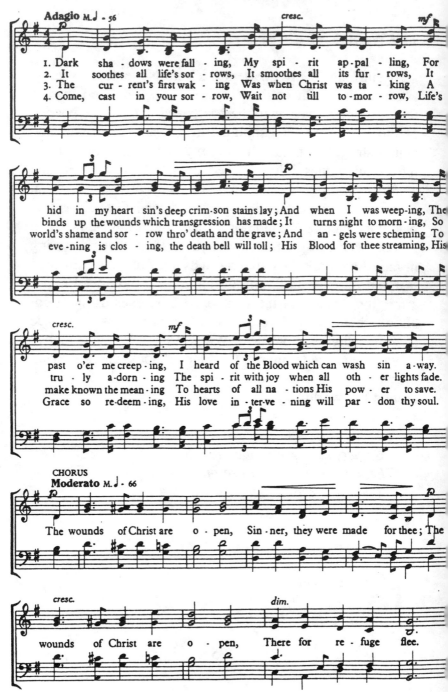

Adagio M. ♩ = 56

1. Dark sha-dows were fall-ing, My spi-rit ap-pal-ling, For
2. It soothes all life's sor-rows, It smoothes all its fur-rows, It
3. The cur-rent's first wak-ing Was when Christ was ta-king A
4. Come, cast in your sor-row, Wait not till to-mor-row, Life's

hid in my heart sin's deep crim-son stains lay; And when I was weep-ing, The
binds up the wounds which transgression has made; It turns night to morn-ing, So
world's shame and sor-row thro' death and the grave; And an-gels were scheming To
eve-ning is clos-ing, the death bell will toll; His Blood for thee streaming, His

past o'er me creep-ing, I heard of the Blood which can wash sin a-way.
tru-ly a-dorn-ing The spi-rit with joy when all oth-er lights fade.
make known the mean-ing To hearts of all na-tions His pow-er to save.
Grace so re-deem-ing, His love in-ter-ve-ning will par-don thy soul.

CHORUS
Moderato M. ♩ = 66

The wounds of Christ are o-pen, Sin-ner, they were made for thee; The

wounds of Christ are o-pen, There for re-fuge flee.

And Yet He Will

I had been visiting in the great Holloway Jail, London. At that time the law forbidding visitors, apart from relations, was inexorable; thus my only means of gaining admittance was to make my appeal in ragged and dilapidated condition as a relative of an inmate. I had talked that day with a man who was serving a sentence which was a very long one. He told me his story. How he once enjoyed the privilege and the happiness of a blessed career as a minister of the Gospel, but sin had crept in little by little until it became his complete master. This is the way sin does. He was a tall man, of exceptionally handsome physique, and I shall never forget the picture of wreckage he presented, standing full height, in his prison clothes, his hand uplifted, as his voice rang out at the close of the story, with the tragic words: "But I fell...I fell...I fell as a star from the heavens to a cinder in hell." And in the memory of this cry, and with the despairing face of the man before me, I wrote the song which I believe has been made a blessing to thousands all over the world, "And Yet He Will Thy Sins Forgive."

And Yet He Will

O Save Me, Dear Lord

Andante M. ♩ = 69

1. I bring Thee my cares and my sor-rows,___ I
2. O Thou Who doth know hu-man frail-ties,___ Pre-
3. For-give all my blind-ness and fol-ly,___ My
4. We thank Thee we find in life's wil-der-ness Es-

bring Thee my doubts and my fears;___ I bring Thee the
-pare me for gain or for loss;___ Tho' born of the
prod-i-gal wan-d'rings and shame.___ Oh, heed now the
-tab-lished Thy gar-dens of grace.___ In temp-ta-tion's

sins which have bur-dened my soul, And sha-dowed my
dust, Lord, our Fa-ther art Thou, The Build-er of
out-cry-ing pains of my heart; I come as the
des-ert a cool sha-ding rock, In dark-ness the

path-way for years. CHORUS
sun and the Cross.___
pro-di-gal came.___ Oh, save me, dear Lord! Oh,
light of Thy Face.___

save me, dear Lord! I plead by Thy mer-cy, Oh, save me, dear Lord!

179

Selected Poems

Taken from Poems By Evangeline Booth (S.A. New York - n.d.)., and miscellaneous other sources.

Stand By The Flag

Stand by the Flag in the thick of the battle!
 Stand by the Flag in the smoke and the flame!
Stand by the Flag when Hell's shot and shell rattle!
 Heed not the pleadings of fear and false shame!
Stand by your colors when others would trample,
 Dragging our Blood-and-Fire emblem in dust.
Stand by the Flag! Be to all an example,
 Faithful till death to your God-given trust.
Stand by the Flag! Let self-interest perish!
 Stand by the Flag--to its principles true!
Stand by the Flag! Love and loyalty cherish!
 Stand by the Yellow, the Red and the Blue!

A Dream

Last night I was dreaming, of Heaven I was dreaming,
I dreamed of my loved ones upon that bright shore;
 I saw their fair faces
 Alight with Heaven's graces,
I heard their sweet voices as in days of yore;
I heard their sweet voices as in days of yore.

I dreamed that with eyes having vision immortal,
I gazed on the ransomed in bright shining bands;
    I heard the grand chorus,
    The anthem so glorious,
The saints wore white robes and had palms in their hands;
The saints wore white robes and had palms in their hands.

I dreamed in this City our wrongs were forgotten,
And friendships once severed became reconciled;
    That hearts pressed by sorrow,
    In that bright tomorrow
Were glad as the angels on whom God had smiled;
Were glad as the angels on whom God had smiled.

I dreamed that the widow, the orphan, the outcast,
Redeemed by Christ's sufferings had reached that bright
shore;
    In one rapturous meeting
    Their loved ones were greeting,
Their sorrows had vanished, their partings were o'er;
Their sorrows had vanished, their partings were o'er.

I dreamed I was listening, in Heaven I was listening,
A voice, much the dearest of voices below,
    Was calling me upward
    To realms bright and glistening,
Was calling my name as in days long ago;
Was calling my name as in days long ago.

The dream of this voice brought loved faces before me,
And up from the past, oh, such fond memories came;

Through every memory
Each a blest sanctuary,
I hear its faint echo still calling my name
I hear its faint echo still calling my name.

Courage

Is it oft thy heart has failed thee?
    Hast thou many times gone back?
Linger not to count the failures
    Strewn along life's stormy track.
If the gathering shadows thicken
    With the voices of the past,
See! there shines a golden promise
    O'er the gloomy darkness cast,
Reading, "As He was with Moses,
    So the Lord will be with thee;"
Reading, "Courage, and with Joshua
    Thou the conqueror shall be."

Dost thou fear to face the perils
    And the shot of battleground?
Oh, remember, in the furnace
    Grace sufficient martyrs found.
Hold not back when storms are raging
    And the enemy is strong,
It is when the Jordan's swelling
    Christ the Pilot leads us on;
As His promise given Moses,
    So His promise given thee,

Fight with courage and with Joshua
    Thou the conqueror shall be.

Courage! Let it be our watchword,
    As a light to guide along,
Over death's last foaming waters,
    Singing then the conqueror's song;
It will brighten up the valley,
    Every shadow penetrate,
It will bring us through life's sorrows,
    It will open wide the gate.
Then in Heaven, through faith triumphant,
    All of life's distresses past,
Then in Heaven "more than conqueror"
    We will gather Home at last.

Old Leaves

Leaves that were once so pretty and young--
They have left the old branches to which they belong
And now on spreads of gold they die;
On the earth's dear breast in state they lie,
Awaiting in shrouds of purple and rose
For the blast of the trumpet the south wind blows.
They, they will rise--immortal they,
Emblem of life's eternal day;
Emblem of flowers, fadeless all;
Emblem of leaves that never fall.
"The Tree of Life," "The Crystal Sea,"
Emblem of soul's immortality.

Loved ones who in resurrection rise
The palm to wave that never dies.
Death, the gate to Heaven above--
Eternal life and the home of love.
O God, we feel the leaves are true--
Thy mercy is eternal too!

Just a Smile

As I've sailed o'er the seas of life's voyage,
    When the billows have swept o'er my bark,
When the winds and the rain tore the foresail in twain
    The course was nigh lost in the dark.
Then the Pilot from out that fair country
    Took the helm and my fears were no more;
Thro' the mists I could see Heaven waiting for me,
    All the lights burning bright on the shore.
Thro' the mists I could see Heaven waiting for me,
    All the lights burning bright on the shore.

There is none like the Heavenly Pilot,
    He will see you safe landed ashore,
When temptation's a gale His great strength will prevail,
    His grace He gives more and more.
Then we'll shout as we sail up the harbor
    By the rays of life's last setting sun;
Oh, glory to God, I'm saved through the Blood,
    Redeemed by the Crucified One!
Oh, glory to God, I'm saved through the Blood,
    Redeemed by the Crucified One!

Just a smile from the face of my Savior dear,
    At the closing up of the day,
With loved ones to wait at the Golden Gate,
    Will take all my troubles away.
Just a welcoming hand with a nailprint there,
    As I lay all my life's burdens down,
Will be more to me than the waving palm,
    More to me than the golden crown.
Will be more to me than the waving palm,
    More to me than the golden crown.

Chapter Eight
Personal Glimpses - Autobiographical

The One Source (Tufts University)

The honor which has today been conferred upon me by this distinguished institution touches my heart deeply, the more so because in its bestowal there is a recognition of some personal effort that I have made in behalf of the world's good.

The appreciation of our fellows of anything we are or have accomplished is a gift beyond all others. It is a gain that cannot be taken or torn from us. It kindles in the heart and memory a light that can alone be extinguished with the life of the individual.

I understand that the original purpose in conferring this degree was to give to the recipient the duty and the privilege of proclaiming publicly that system of knowledge embraced in the Faculty of Arts--a privilege and a duty which I have exercised from my youth up--and it is a great happiness for me to receive, even at this late date, from such an authoritative source the justification of this assumed prerogative.

This particular degree has reference to science and to philosophy rather than to theology, medicine, or law. The objective of science and philosophy is, or ought to be, the greatest possible good to the greatest possible number. The achievements of science and philosophy are knowledge and wisdom. From my earliest years I have been taught that all knowledge and all wisdom are found in their fullest expression in the person of our Lord and Savior Jesus Christ, and from my earliest years I have believed that in directing men to Him I was directing them to the Fountainhead of all wisdom.

Because of this I was led to consecrate my every power--physical, mental and spiritual--to this service, without any thought as to honor, or in the smallest degree soliciting the praise of men.

Yet I have not been without ambition. My father, at the conclusion of an interview with the late King Edward, said, "Your Majesty, some men's passion is art, some men's passion is fame, some men's passion is gold, but my passion is man!"

And I am ever seeking to place my feet in the footprints he has trailed across the sands of time. My greatest ambition, my highest thought, my tenderest prayer, the very zenith of my aspirations, journeying with me through the years have been that I, by the merits of God's grace and the Cross of Calvary, might be accounted worthy to stand with my father and mother, arrayed as they shall be arrayed, before His throne upon the gladdest Morning the world will have ever seen.

Whether it was that my birth was on Christmas Day, or that that Christmas Day happened to be the Sabbath, or that the home in which I was born was next to a church, where the chime of the bells called the people to worship; whether these events cast their shadows before them, marking the way I was to pass, I cannot say.

I would rather think it was the ineffaceable impression made upon my awakening soul one deeply solemn night when my mother taking me by the hand, led me out under the great canopy of the skies, and pointing up to the stars, those gems that brighten night's sable throne, told me the

188

story that has come down through the ages of the Star and the Scepter blazing a path to that holy place where intermingled the great and the small, the learned and the simple, wise men's robes and shepherds' smocks, that awakened within my soul a thirst to illumine, in some measure, as one of those stars, the darkness of this world.

The spirit of my prayer was that the light within me might be but the reflection of a glory that was not my own, shining with penetrating rays--the rays of truth, of justice, of goodness, of worthiness of soul; that God, through me, should reveal men's souls unto themselves, that they, seeing sin in all its hideous reality, might turn from it and live; that I, like that Star over Bethlehem, might mark the way to the hallowed spot where the weary may find rest; to the rugged cross where the sin-laden wanderer can lay down his burden; to the Source of all life where the desolate of heart, the broken in hope, the fallen by the way shall find their everlasting peace. Then the purpose of God in my having come into the world would be achieved.

I felt then, and I feel now, that whatever charms, or riches, or earthly possessions, or the admiration or love of mankind, might come to me as a result of a kindly interest in my fellows, these would be but as accumulated ashes, the fires of their value burnt out, apart from my life through grace having proved to be a star shining through the vast expanse of men's souls and lighting them to God.

This ambition, in my early days, led me to put aside my customary dress and clothe myself in rags that I might reach the lowest and darkest in the lowest and darkest places, those where the bodies and the souls of men struggle against unutterable conditions and unmasterable miseries and go down.

And as I have come along the journey I have been required to make sacrifices of things infinitely precious to the human heart. But, oh, the vast reward! I have seen violence conquered by smiles, obstinacy by tolerance, ignorance by truth, anger by gentleness.

I have seen the black holes of superstition and ignorance illumined by the downflashing of revelation. I have seen the satanic powers of hideous cruelty, barbarous injustice and wanton oppression surrender to the ministry of kindness. I have seen exacting extortion fall before pity for "him that hath none to help him."

I have seen intellects, armed with the assured impregnable defenses of infidel argument, that have ventured to question the immovable, unalterable fact that God is, stripped of their strength by the simple faith of a little child.

Ladies and gentlemen, there is only one law for all government, one panacea for all ill, one redress for all wrong, and that is love of God.

The man that lives in the practice of virtue, in the worship of God, in the pursuit of righteousness, contributes riches of inestimable worth to the uplift of the world.

But let me say (Dr. Cousens, I hope it will not be out of place) I feel I cannot close this address without an appeal to all to turn their eyes to the one Source from which flows that which alone can ennoble any calling or any vocation. We cannot live without Him. What, without His guiding hand, is life? What, without His enrichment, can be true treasure? What, without His blessing, can abide permanently? More and more is the language of my heart:

A boat at midnight sent alone
  To drift upon a moonless sea,
A flute whose leading chord is gone,
A wounded bird, that hath but one
Imperfect wing to soar upon,
  Are like what I am, without Thee!

Believing in your sympathy with me in the work to which I have set my hand, I can only ask that you pray for me that I may be kept strong in courage, unfaltering in constancy, untrammeled in belief in God, with a faith radiant in the sunrise of an eternal dawn.

My Covenant

An address of Acceptance by Evangeline Booth, delivered in London on the occasion of her election by the High Council as General of The Salvation Army. September 4, 1934

From The Officers' Review (International Headquarters, London), January-February 1935.

I stand before you trembling, not with the honor conferred upon me--although I think I sense this to the full--but trembling with the wakening realization of the tremendous obligations you have called me to meet in electing me your General of the world-wide Salvation Army.

As you know, I began my service to God at a very early age, and as you also know, I have lived a long life, not one hour of which has been spent out of the Army.

As it is with most of those who have desired to accomplish great things, I have struggled with a painful sense of the limitations of my natural gifts.

But I think I can say here this morning, to the glory of Christ whose love "constraineth us," that if any one has witnessed effort multiplied a hundred-fold, if any one has seen adversity bring forth blessing, if any one has beheld a small thing assume influences and powers that were mighty, surely it is I!

God has been good to me. In times when I could not see His face, He has been good to me. He has kept in my

192

soul a steadfastness of faith that has brought down through the years that compelling force which predominates, influences and permeates all beside--that force, the master passion of the cross!

While I take this election to indicate that I am chosen of God and of you to be your General, I discern in this elevation the injunction of our Lord Himself:

"Whosoever will be great among you, let him be your minister; and whosoever will be chief among you, let him be your servant."

These words constrain me here this morning to make a covenant with you, that you may know something of what is my thought as to my service to you.

By the constraint of His love, I will serve you in a ministry of holiness, joyful and earnest, and all-compelling in moral power.

I will seek to proclaim the old truths with new energy and with a new vitality.

I will seek to preach among you the truth as it is in Christ Jesus. Not with faltering tongue, or unsound or questionable teaching, but I will preach it as the Apostles of old preached it: the one controlling principle of the soul; the one motive power; mighty in life, the source of all morals, the inspiration of all charity, the sanctification of every relationship and the sweetness of every toil.

I will preach it with a heart of constancy that will change not.

I will preach it in the spirit of prayer, that I may minister unto you Divine aid.

Every impulse of my being shall be to this end. Every talent I possess, every physical, mental and spiritual gift with which God has endowed me, I consecrate to this one purpose.

I will ask no privileges, I will seek no honors, I will accept no benefits, I will look for no friends but such as will help me to minister to you--the leaders of the Army at the different points of our world-embracing battlefield--a ministry that will help you to bring the Kingdom of God on earth in the hearts and lives of men.

I will give no time, I will expend no energies, I will not even pray prayers that will not help me to help you to bring the Kingdom of God on earth in the hearts and lives of men.

I will be among you also "as one that serveth." You shall not find me lacking in rendering you separately, or as a body, together with those dear to you, any service of which I am capable that is in harmony with your high calling and with my office.

But, standing upon my knowledge of the all-sufficient grace of our Lord Jesus Christ, I do not hesitate also to promise that in every sense I will be to you a leader in the great trust which your choice has imposed upon me.

You will ever find me in the front. You will find me in the foremost line of our warfare's most heated conflict, whatever form that conflict may take.

Whether it be seeking to unravel the knotty entanglements of the sorest problems of my executive office; whether it be along the firing-line of attack upon the enemies of Christ on public fields; or whether it be in the position of butting off the shell and shot of harm to our organization, or to our humblest soldiery, I am determined that none shall be before me. None shall surpass me in toil. None shall surpass me in sacrifice. None shall surpass me in abandonment of self.

Here this morning, with prayerful deliberation, in the presence of this important assembly, and in the presence of God, I dedicate every power I possess, for life or for death, to the stupendous obligation of filling the office to which I am called, with fidelity, with purity, and with wisdom, so that the blessed life-giving streams of our organization shall reach farther points; shall be more widely spread, and that our Army, in this day of strife and struggle, political upheaval, economic distresses and human sorrows, shall sound forth to the world with a more clarion note than ever before the trumpets of "peace on earth" and "Glory to God in the highest."

Now I have made my Covenant, what about you?

What is it I ask of you?

I repeat the words of Jehu: "Is thine heart right, as my heart is with thy heart? If it be, then give me thine hand." (2 Kings 10:15).

I want you all with me. Not one omitted.

I want you all closely with me. Nothing between.

Undividedly with me. No reservations. Wholesouledly with me. Nothing withheld.

If all are friends in this room but one, then I have one friend too few. Let not a single heart be set against me.

This General arrangement is the nearest to the marriage altar I have ever come. You have taken me for "better or for worse." Now try me, and see how much "better" you will find me, and how little "worse." If more worse than you expect it won't last long.

But do not let any one set his heart against me before I get started!

All our hearts must be set one with the other, against every evil thing that would hurt the Army. We know that by union the smallest things become great; and by discord the greatest things are destroyed.

I can never find time for sight-seeing. Perhaps I am stupid in this way, or, I should say, perhaps this is one of the ways in which I am stupid.

I have been thirty years in the United States, but not any of the physical features of renown of that great country have I visited--not even Niagara Falls, or that marvelous, unparalleled grandeur of nature, the Grand Canyon, or the other sights which visitors come from all parts of the world to look up. I simply could not take the time from my work.

But I did have the pleasure of spending three days in Switzerland a few years ago, and for the first time looked upon the glory and majesty of the Alps.

As I lifted my eyes to their snow-crowned summits, I observed that the greatest impression made upon me was not that of the isolated mountain peak of Jungfrau lifting her lovely head clear into the sky. It was that made by the colossal dimensions of the whole range of mountains.

I trembled with emotion as I gazed upon their mighty shoulders, erect in each other's strength, shining in the light reflected from each other's sunbathed faces, and in their billowing structure appearing to lean upon each other's support.

It can never pass from my vision, the sight of them.

So it is with us in this room. We are as a range of mountains. We must all tower together. If one mountain-peak is a little higher than the rest, it is only for the glory of the whole.

We must stand together shoulder to shoulder, and present to the world one vast mountain-range of righteousness and truth, robed with the snow-white mantle of "Holiness unto the Lord."

Evangeline's Four Adopted Children

A most diligent search of the voluminous archives revealed no existing letters to her four adopted children: Dorothy, Jai, Pearl and Willie. However, the Railton Centre in Toronto produced several photos, some of which we have included. There are scattered references to the children in various publications.

The War Cry (Toronto, July 31, 1897) describes their involvement in a Good Friday meeting, as follows:

"As each section of the cross was added, Dot sang a well-chosen chorus which emphasized the point which the Commissioner had brought out, as well as introduced a diversion to avoid a strain upon the audience's beautiful attention.

"Willie and Pearl sang several choruses to the great delight of the audience, which liberally applauded them. Everybody fell in love with them at first sight. Are they not a forcible object-lesson of what training may do with the pliable lives of children? Many kindly remarks were made by the people about the children; certainly the sincerest form of praise and recognition of the Commissioner's care, patience, and love so freely given to the development and multiplying of the best emotions and abilities."

The Toronto World (n.d.) describes a meeting in Massey Hall:

"The Commissioner's little adopted children, Willie and Pearl, began the service by one of them singing in a sweet, childish voice to the accompaniment of the auto-harp, played by the other...'I think when I read that sweet story of old.'"

Earlier references to two of the children are found in Booth-Tucker's "Life of Catherine Booth." At the Army Mother's bedside during her last illness, mention is made of "Dot and Jai, in whom Mrs. Booth had been deeply interested for several years."

To a group of children, she said, "The next time you see me, I shall be in a glorified body with white and shining robes. I shall look out for you and Dot and Jai in heaven."

The story continues:

"Dot was speechless with grief. During the earlier stages of Mrs. Booth's illness, she had been allowed to wait on her, arranging her medicines, or running messages, and interesting her with her childish prattle. But now that she had come to say her last goodbye, her little heart, usually so buoyant, seemed too full for language. But the tears that filled her eyes spoke for her."

Jai responded quite differently:

"With practical forethought, little Jai, who was about four years old, had armed himself with a toy musical box, thinking it would help to cheer and soothe the sufferer, and producing it from under his pinafore, while his large dark eyes peered inquiringly into Mrs. Booth's face, he said, 'I would play a little music to you, Mrs. Booth, I would, only I'm afraid it would make you worser! But I have been praying for you, and when you are gone to heaven, I am going to take care of my mother, I am.' (Miss Eva Booth had been his special guardian, and he had been accustomed to call her 'Mother.') "'And when I get old, I shall be a major, and I'll get lots of souls saved,' trying with childish instinct to comfort her with what he knew would please her most. And who can tell to what extent the ambition thus implanted in childhood shall hereafter bear fruit in lives of fullest consecration and wholehearted service!"

Another interesting allusion to Jai was discovered in the London War Cry (December 6, 1890):

"Commissioner Miss Booth at a recent meeting in England said she had a bad throat and every word uttered gave her pain. That was the reason she could not address them at length that evening, but she had an able Lieutenant in little Jai, a Swiss boy, age 4 years, whom she had adopted when he was only six months old.

"Little Jai then mounted a chair and sang several favorite hymns. He accompanied his singing with swinging his arms in true Salvation Army fashion. When the end of the verse was finished, he called 'altogether!' in such a

200

commanding tone that many who would not otherwise have sung joined in the chorus with all their hearts under such a youthful leader."

What happened to these four children in later years? Pearl was promoted to Glory in Buffalo as Mrs. Lt. Colonel Arthur Woodruff, after tending to her mother during Evangeline's last illness. In an interview later, Lt. Colonel Woodruff suggested that Willie was killed during World War I. No information has been discovered on Dot or Jai. However, there is no doubt about the importance of these four children in the life of their adopted mother, Evangeline Booth.

Letter to American Comrades and Friends

Upon her appointment to the American command.

From The War Cry (New York), December 17, 1904.

My Dear Comrades and Friends:

At our honored General's command, I am to fill the important position of your leader and comrade in the glorious Salvation contest in which you are enlisted. In stepping to the appointment, perhaps I need not say how greatly I am impressed by the magnitude of the undertaking, the immensity of its proportions, the vastness of its opportunities, the weight of its responsibility and the grace, strength and ingenuity required for its successful prosecution.

Then I cannot help but say I am keenly conscious of the poverty of my own abilities for the fulfillment of the great task, which sense is enhanced by the knowledge I possess of the unique gifts of your late beloved Commander-in-Chief. To follow one so laborious, so self-sacrificing, endowed with such inventive genius, demonstrated in multifarious schemes and methods for the salvation of the people, the amelioration of sorrow and the relief of want, is in itself a difficult task. But I am reckoning upon the inspiration of his example remaining with you, and that the spirit he has instilled into your hearts will ensure the heartiest cooperation with my own ambitions and desires, so that we shall not only maintain every new enterprise already on foot, but stretch out still further in the same field of Salvation philanthropy, and so gratify the Commander's heart by realizing to a greater degree the hopes he had entertained.

Then there is one who poured out her life in your midst; my glorified sister, your glorified leader. Her choice attributes of intellect and soul, her gifts of tongue, and pen and heart; her brave soldiership, her wonderful womanhood, have all made great lights which can never be dimmed, up and down the stretches of your vast country. Tens of thousands have been enriched for earth and heaven by the beauty of her influence; our own souls have again and again been quickened and inspired by her blest teachings, and although now lifted from the scene of active struggle, from the field of desperate fighting, her devotion and self-sacrifice, her words of love and wisdom, are still with us, strengthening up our hearts in the hard, long pull to make the Blest Shore.

You and I were peculiarly one in the great sorrow of her leaving us. She belonged to the American field by ten thousand fond and special ties; she was mine by the sacred bonds of flesh and blood, and a sister's quenchless love. We have both lost her--yet, in a much surer and safer place than earth, we both have her.

While I cannot lay claim to all the gifts possessed by my predecessors, yet I can, by faith in our Lord and Savior, assure you that in toil, in sacrifice, in prayers, in being instant in season and out of season, in ceaseless endeavor to promote the further happiness and usefulness of my people, in effort to uplift the poor and save the lost, in love strong and changeless, you shall not find me wanting.

I come to you in full recognition and appreciation of the victories you have already recorded. You have battled bravely for the establishment and maintenance of the Army; you have borne many burdens; you have been loyal under strong temptations; you have held on in the face of a thousand foes, and today you stand an invincible band for God and right.

I come to you in the fullness of sympathy for future warfare. Every shot you fire will have the backing of my prayers; every struggle you are engaged in will be interlaced with my ambitions for your triumph; every sorrow that comes to you will wake pain in my own heart; every joy that lightens your spirit will cast sunshine across my own way. Your difficulties, your disappointments, your hard battles and your victories and your happiness will always have me in them, because my sympathy will be with you.

I come to you, not only with a passionate love for sinners, and a tender pity for them, but with a strong faith, which can unflinchingly, and without exception, believe for their salvation. I believe that those who are the lowest down can be lifted up by the Omnipotent Arm of God: those who are the furthest out on the roughest road can come home by the way of the all-forgiving love of God; that those lost in the black darkness of doubt and unbelief can find their way out by the Lamp, the shining Gospel lamp, the light of God.

I come to you determined to put forth every effort to save the precious children. They crowd our path, they fill our homes, they are the everlasting song or endless dirge of parent hearts. They hold infinite possibilities for good or evil. Apart from what we can do for them, tens of thousands are hopeless, helpless, defenseless. We must find them, we must protect them, we must save them.

I come to you with heated ambitions to assist you with your numerous schemes for the alleviation of the poor. The misery, the hunger, the pains of the destitute have pressed my soul from a small child. I shall glory in the opportunity the American command will offer to marshal relief columns into the darkness of your great cities and rescue the victims of poverty and despair.

I come in the name of the Lord God Almighty to lead you on, to establish what is already begun, to strengthen what is weak, to encourage what is timid, to persuade to the front the feet that lag behind, and by power divine, grace limitless, love boundless, and strength omnipotent triumph in triumphs greater than anything seen or dreamed about in your land. Here and now for the purpose I place all that is within me upon God's altar. Every faculty of my mind I marshal for this assault; every energy of my being I enlist in this cause; every passion of my soul I consecrate to this theme. I shall live for this, I shall work for this, I shall believe for this; that He may make me a great blessing to you.

But I must ask your cooperation, your love, and your confidence. I shall crave for this, I cannot help doing so. My dear and faithful people in my late command have given it to me with a generosity that has surpassed expectations. It has been my stronghold in times of stress and suffering. I cannot help but hope it may be the same with you. In fact, when I look toward the great battle that is before me, I ask it of you, that you will rally around me, that you will follow after me, that you will stand close beside me, and that you will trust me. Day by day, does God spare me, I shall seek to serve you so as to merit it.

In closing I would say I think you know that already I love you. We first met in battle, in the rattle of shot and burst of shell, and nothing can so quickly weave the web which fastens hearts together as the whirling loom of hardship, loss and trial, and so our hearts became linked up; let it suffice to say that the thundering, hammering, grinding experiences of nearly nine years' war have not severed the threads.

Leaning upon the Arm of Omnipotence and sheltered 'neath the Wing of the Almighty, I pray that we may prove ourselves valiant in battle, fulfil the will of God and gratify the desires of the world-wide heart of our honored General.

Yours for this end.

Evangeline Booth

Letters to Her Divisional Commanders

As Commander-in-Chief in the United States, Evangeline wrote frequently to her Divisional Commanders on a variety of personal and official concerns.

Here are a few examples.

National Headquarters
120 West 14 Street
New York

August 14, 1926

Personal
E.C.B.

Major and Mrs. Waldron
204 Federal Street
Portland, Maine

My dear Major and Mrs. Waldron,

Now that I have sufficiently recovered to do a little dictating, my first and strongest impulse is to send some expression from my heart to my leading officers, the Divisional Commanders. I shall, of course, be making an attempt to voice my thanks through *The War Cry* for the many expressions of thought and sympathy which have reached my sick room during my long and severe illness, but to you I must send a personal word as well.

I have never been so low; I have never suffered so much; I have never been so far removed from all interest in the things of this world. There were many times when it seemed to me that the only chain that held me back was my love for my people and the love of my people for me, and the thought that you might miss me and need me if I left you just yet.

Therefore the expressions of your sincere sympathy and heart feeling for me which reached me during my illness and were read to me by Colonel Griffith when I was able to hear them, without doubt brought to bear upon me the strongest influences to hold me here.

To say I thank you and that I shall never be able to forget your quick and tender sympathy poorly expresses how greatly strengthened is the bond of comradeship and friendship between us, or how heavily my heart is weighted with desire and ambition to be with you again that I may serve you with a truer devotion and a greater abandonment to the interests of our blessed warfare.

While still considerably below my normal condition of health yet I am every day making progress in my climb upward. I know you will continue to pray for me. I want strength and health and nerve energy that I may be able to work hard and long and continuously to lighten the burdens of you all.

I send you both my love. You may depend upon me more than ever for a higher leadership and a truer comradeship.

Your Commander to serve you,

Evangeline Booth
COMMANDER

National Headquarters
120 West 14 Street
New York

December 1, 1928

Personal
E.C.B.

Major John Waldron,
Scranton, Pa.

My dear Major:

I want to write you a few personal lines upon the calling of the High Council.

The receipt of your message, revealing your deep interest and unwavering confidence truly brought me exceptional encouragement, the more so because the sentiments you express with regard to the subject exercising the minds of all officers at the present time are characteristic of those held by the Staff from sea to sea of this great country. Perhaps there has never been a moment in my entire career when I have so warmly appreciated the love and trust of my foremost officers as today, for there has never been a time in my entire career that I have needed this assurance so sorely.

You evidently apprehend my personal anxiety owing to the continued and serious sickness of the General. For the improvement experienced we must all thank God while we continue to pray that, if it be the divine Will, his critical condition may soon pass, giving us ground for a more hopeful outlook that will ultimately result in complete recovery.

I fear the summoning of the High Council is not quite understood by some. This action--you should know and tell any of your officers and soldiers who might question it--is in perfect harmony with the provisions of the Constitution. The possibility of just such an emergency as that which now arises through the General's prolonged ill-health has been amply provided for in our Deed Poll by the Founder; and the High Council--viz. all the active commissioners and Territorial Commanders--is charged with the responsibility of adjudicating upon any disability that questions the General's fitness to fulfill the duties of his great office.

Should the judgment of the Council confirm the medical testimony and the common observation of the past months, then it will become obligatory upon the Council to make some provision for the effective occupancy of the High Command, that the work of the Army universal be not only not hindered but advanced with all the necessary urgency.

Vital questions have been before the General for many months, all attention to which has been precluded by this unfortunate and deplored sickness. It is very strongly felt in the highest circles of the Army that some solution to these problems must be found in order that the glorious oneness of this Movement shall be preserved and its mighty progress assured. Hence the calling of the High Council.

I was particularly glad to have your message--indeed it was necessary to me--because I go not alone to speak my own conscience upon this and the vitally important question of a change in the method of making safe the successorship of our present and future Generals, but I go as the Ambassador for the Army in the United States to represent you and to speak for yours. Therefore, you will realize the impetus it has brought me to know that I am well supported, as every Staff Officer within the precincts of my command has assured me.

I know you will pray for the General, pray for the Council and pray for me. Pray that grace and wisdom and strength divine may be given to us as individuals and all as a body.

Again thanking you for your ever appreciated confidence, I am as always

Yours depending upon you,

Evangeline Booth
COMMANDER

P.S. Do not be persuaded that there is any dissension or strife within the ranks. Everything is calm and trustful. In fact, unmistakable evidence has come to me from all quarters that our officers are with all energy going on with their work.

E.C.B.

National Headquarters
120 West 14 Street
New York

June 22, 1931

Personal
E.C.B.

Brigadier John Waldron,
128-130 Penn Avenue,
Scranton, Pa.

My dear Brigadier:

As you will imagine, I arrived back in New York pretty well tired out. The welcome was simply marvelous. I do not think there has ever been anything like it in the Army's history.

The love of the people was demonstrated in every possible form, and the conservatism which usually prevails in this city was for once utterly forgotten in the laughter and cheers and tears of thousands upon thousands who thronged the entire block on Fourteenth Street between Sixth and Seventh Avenues.

Since then there has come upon me the pent-up tide of business and correspondence accumulated during my absence.

But why bother you with what you will know? I write only to express the biggest thanks of which I am capable for the splendid thing you gave me in your division. You have thrown on the pages of my experience some of the most remarkable scenes--crowds, blessed evidences of the presence of God--in the open street that I have ever known.

You must have worked, and worked hard, and kept on working to inspire the officers concerned to the degree necessary to bring all this about.

Please accept the deep and lasting appreciation of your Commander's heart. These things you have accomplished will never pass from my memory, and will never be bereft of the thankfulness that will continue to well up within me.

Please give my love to dear Mrs. Waldron.

Yours more than ever depending upon you,

Evangeline Booth
COMMANDER

National Headquarters
120 West 14th Street
New York

July 30, 1934

Personal
E.C.B.

Brigadier John Waldron
128 Penn Avenue
Scranton, Pa.

My dear Brigadier:

Now that I am approaching the time for my departure
for London, with the important mission of attending the
High Council, I want to send my Divisional Commanders
a special few words direct from myself, first asking your
prayers, and secondly, to tell you that although I shall have
much to think about and much of an anxious nature, I shall
remember you in thought and in prayer.

During the absence of your Commissioner and my own
absence it will be more necessary for you to exercise even
greater alertness in watching the affairs relative to your
Command, and put forth even a more determined effort to
keep everything on the move forward, so that there shall be
no part of our operations that will suffer because each
Territory's leader and myself will be away from our
respective positions. In this I am sure you will agree with

me, and I know you well enough to feel confident that there will be no slackening of your energies or withholding of the best you have to give.

The years you have been with me have well convinced me of your whole-souled consecration to the Kingdom of God under our Flag, and too, your service has assured me beyond doubt, of not only your loyal devotion to me personally but your fervent desire to meet my wishes and fulfil my hopes concerning you and your work. Therefore, I leave you for a season with every confidence that your part of the work shall not suffer, but that if anything it shall profit because of your more strenuous endeavors to force the march forward in every respect.

I ask your prayers. I ask that they may be strong and believing on my behalf, for my judgment will be sought and depended upon regarding the most intricate questions concerning our Army, and I shall hourly need the guidance and the light of the wisdom of God.

Before I start I look for the coming home to my Command in this land, that has showered upon me such love and unsurpassed following. God bless you much. If His will should compel me to take a higher place, I shall need your prayers the more and shall depend upon your love the more.

Yours as always under the Flag,

Evangeline Booth
COMMANDER-IN-CHIEF

P.S. It will please me to get an acknowledgment to this letter before I sail on the Leviathan on August 11th.

We are Soldiers of The Love that Overcomes Hatred

General Evangeline Booth's farewell message to all Salvationists, upon her retirement from active service.

From The War Cry (New York), October 28, 1939.

My dear Officers, Soldiers and Friends of The Salvation Army throughout the World:

It is all but impossible for me to find words that will adequately express the overwhelming emotions of my heart now that the time has come to bid you farewell as your General.

I need not assure you that you are inexpressibly dear to me. You have given me a noble support. Your love for me has been generous. We have had many happy years of association. Your near-flattering loyalty, your unwavering confidence, the sympathy you have showered upon me in seasons of particular trial and heavy sorrow; these are the treasures I take with me into retirement. They are your gift. They are more to me than any money could buy, and with a never-dying gratitude I praise the God of all Grace whose Holy Spirit has been so abundantly shed abroad in your hearts.

Always I have been conscious of falling short of my own standards and ideals, which sense of insufficiency has frequently been a cause of deep disquiet within me. It is the Lord Himself, and only the Lord, who has enabled me

218

to be of service to you. And this service has been rendered in the fullness of an undying love. The best that is in me-- that has been my willing and eager response to Him who claims nothing less than our best.

What an indisputable declaration is my life of the truth of God's promise to magnify the sacrifice, no matter how small and poor, that is laid upon His altar. With tears in my eyes, I look again in memory into the faces of those in different parts of the world who were brought into The Army under my leadership. There are not a few who were trained under me at Clapton. I glory in the remembrance that some of you who will read these words were led to the Savior through my ministration of the Gospel. With happiness in my heart, I claim you as "my children in the Gospel." Your witness, your labors, your faith are my exceeding great reward, and deep is the joy I find in your never-forgotten names.

During the past four and a half years all of you, without distinction, under the Flag of the Army, have been in a very special sense my trust. I have felt it to be my most sacred obligation to care for your well-being, spiritual and temporal, with watchful tenderness and oversight. I have not permitted the great responsibilities of this vast organization to prevent my entering into your joys with a true jubilance, and sharing your sorrows with a deep and understanding sympathy.

How often I have had the choice privilege of blessing your little children! How often the passing of our dearly beloved has found us close together in our tears! How often in the disappointments and troubles of hearth and home we have come to a dearer understanding! Together we have marched forth, shoulder to shoulder, and fought the good fight of faith on ten thousand fields of battle.

By the will of God and the choice of The Army, I was called to be unto you a shepherd. Let me remind you that I was appointed to a position of leadership only after I had learned obedience as a true Soldier of The Salvation Army, wholly abandoned to the call of our warfare, as ready to die as to live, a willing sacrifice on the altar of our great Army's sacred purposes and traditions.

Accepting without reservation the unalterable principles of The Army, I have sought by God's help never to permit weariness, or discouragement, or the condemnation of others to hinder my using to the best of my ability the divine opportunities which arise for every one of us under the folds of the Blood and Fire flag. Hour by hour, day by day, year by year, I have prayed for that spiritual strength that would enable me to be in truth a leader, first in toil, first in sacrifice, with the spirit of willingness, bearing fruit in deeds of holy daring in things temporal and eternal.

Therefore I leave with you, with the hope that it may help you, my conception of the most holy calling by which we are called to our commission of Officers and to our duty as Soldiers of The Salvation Army.

What are the "hidden treasures of grace" that may be ours if we meditate on the higher purposes of God's will revealed by His Spirit to all who humbly seek His wisdom as the guide to the life and health of the soul? By what weapons do we go forth undaunted to meet our foe, bitter, implacable and terrible in his constantly resurgent rage?

GOD IS LOVE, and we who serve God are known by the love we bear to others. We can never have too much of love in our lives, for <u>Love is the superabundance of Life</u>. As Salvationists we are soldiers of the love that overcomes hatreds, that overflows into the emptiness of the loveless and the unlovable, that heals all wounds, that comforts all sorrows, that wins back the wanderer to the Father's home.

GOD IS TRUTH, the breastwork that is a bulwark around the heart of love, impregnable against the evasions, deception, subterfuges, allurements, flatteries and temptations that assail a soldier of the cross as he confronts the influences of an environing world. He who goes forth daily wearing the breastplate of Truth, burnished with a glowing sincerity, is secure whatever be the artillery of evil that may scatter death-dealing munitions as he advances.

GOD IS RIGHTEOUS. He saves the sinner. He does not condone the sin. It is His righteousness, not our own, that is buckled on to our arm as a shield of faith, and worn on our brow as a helmet of salvation. <u>We stand erect because we stand for all right, whatever it may be, against all wrong</u>. Not by a hair's-breadth do we swerve from the eternal and absolute justice of God as the only alternative to cruel injustices in the world around us. On the cross Jesus vindicated that justice; and justice, the Magna Carta of the weak amid the strong, and the rule of personal character, is the foundation of His Kingdom.

In the unending conflict against sin, and the shame and sorrow that arc the shadows of sin, wc fight with spiritual weapons. The only sword that is sharp enough to pierce deep and straight into the vitals of iniquity is the Sword of the Spirit, <u>which is the Word of God</u>. There is no right save where the hearts of men are right.

The Spirit within us awakens every sanctified human power. We fight on our knees. We fight in the trenches. We fight in the hospitals. We fight in the prisons. We fight gambling. We fight intoxicating liquor. We fight vice. We fight whatever it be that wastes lives for which Christ died. We fight for the rescue and redemption of whatever in life has been lost. And there is no discharge in this war. I have spent my life fighting, and I know of no other way to spend my life. I must fight to the end or perish.

<u>My dear Officers and Comrades, I once more call you to your Bible</u>. Upon its pages I have found infinite wisdom and infinite love. Between its covers are the mind and heart of God. For over sixty years the Bible has been the food of my soul, my discipline, my encouragement, my education and my message. If you neglect your Bible you perpetrate a great wrong to your spiritual life.

<u>We hold nothing back</u>. In this hour of farewell, my dear Comrades and Friends of every land, I think that in all humility I may use the words of the Apostle Paul when he said: "I have not shunned to declare unto you the whole counsel of God."

If there be any truth about God, or Jesus Christ and His atoning sacrifice on the cross, about death and judgment, that I have not made known to all who have listened to me, I pray that I may be forgiven. But I beg you to tell me what it is.

And let me add that the responsibility of each of you, according to the knowledge that God has given you and your powers of expression, is no different from that which I have tried to fulfil. Shun not, I plead with you, to declare the whole counsel of God, for nothing less than this is adequate to the desperate need of man for whose salvation we received our commission to testify to the power of the cross.

When I was appointed International General my first charge to you was, <u>Preach the Gospel of Jesus Christ</u>! My last word as your General is again, <u>Preach the Gospel of Jesus Christ</u>! Let no man make you afraid. Clear your souls of the blood of all men. Preach Christ not merely as a gracious ornament of civilization, to be admired and accepted or not, at will, but as the Supreme Gift to a world lost without Him. The Risen Christ, triumphant over the tomb, and all the sin that brought Him to the tomb. Preach salvation in Christ as that which we must have or perish

Oh, my Comrades and Friends, my heart is enlarged towards you as I commend you to the leadership of the new International General. I have known him for many years. I am wholly confident that his entire being is abandoned utterly to your welfare, spiritual and temporal; that he has no higher thought than your good and through you the good of the world. As you proceed to new and greater conquests through Him who loved us and gave Himself for us, I pray for you unceasingly.

Officers, Locals, Bandmasters, Bandsmen, Soldiers--all-- <u>quit you like men</u>! The storm may break upon you. Do not turn aside from its fury. Head straight into the tempest with a holy determination that nothing shall release your hand from its grip. <u>Hold fast to that which has taken hold of you, the strong hand of an all-conquering Savior.</u>

Farewell!   I leave you with an inevitable sense of separation.   I know this day what Paul meant when he wrote the imperishable words that I now leave with you:

I thank my God upon every remembrance of you: always in every prayer of mine for you all making request with joy, for your fellowship in the Gospel from the first day until now; even as it is meet to think this of you all, because I have you in my heart; inasmuch as in the defence and confirmation of the Gospel, ye are partakers with me of grace.   For God is my record how greatly I long after you all with the affection of Christ Himself.